21 REASONS CREATIVITY IS LIKE SEX

Why everyone can do it, have a sense of humor about it, and use it to make the world a better place.

Written and designed by
Courtney Smith Kramer

All Emoji art supplied by EmojiOne

If you
don't laugh
during sex
at least once,
you're having
sex with
the wrong
person.

To my parents and kids, fair warning I talk about sex in this book.

To my husband, Bryan, thank you for always supporting me and being by my side (and underneath and on top).

To serendipity, for leading me through this journey and into unknown, fucking scary but really, really gratifying territory.

EGO IS THE CREATIVITY KILLER.

Creativity is your manifestation of self. The ego is its counterpart, there to balance it, and they have to work in concert. Each were created to work together, but like the fine line between love and hate, they can turn on each other and sabotage each's purpose.

Anytime the ego takes over, we see jealousy, greed, oppression and criticism. Sometimes, if people feel threatened, they'll criticize an idea to tear it down, only to make themselves feel better. That's all ego. Creativity is the complete opposite of that. It's the openness and willingness to share, and to give the best of yourself in a way that is very non-threatening, and in cooperation with everybody.

 Courtney Smith Kramer That looks like how Minions were created.
Like · Reply · 👍 1 · 3 hrs

 **Jay Baer** ✓ LOL
Like · Reply · 👍 1 · 3 hrs

 Warren Whitlock Minions do it in a box
Like · Reply · 1 hr

CONTENTS

LIFE'S CREATIVE CIRCLE.

THE most popular conception of creativity is that it's something to do with the arts.

Nonsense.

Creativity is imagination, and imagination is for everyone.

Use this wheel to help you understand life's creative circle.

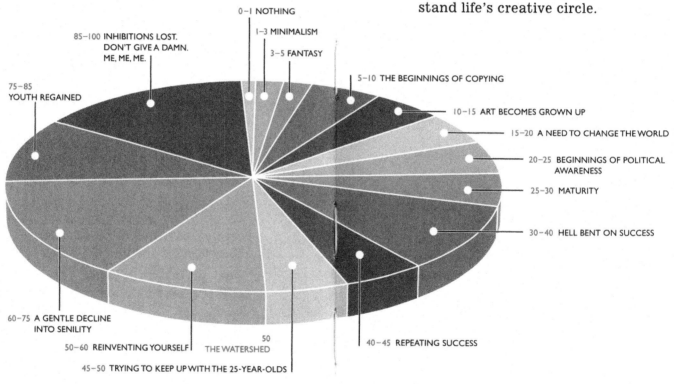

0–1 NOTHING

1–3 MINIMALISM

3–5 FANTASY

5–10 THE BEGINNINGS OF COPYING

10–15 ART BECOMES GROWN UP

15–20 A NEED TO CHANGE THE WORLD

20–25 BEGINNINGS OF POLITICAL AWARENESS

25–30 MATURITY

30–40 HELL BENT ON SUCCESS

40–45 REPEATING SUCCESS

50 THE WATERSHED

45–50 TRYING TO KEEP UP WITH THE 25-YEAR-OLDS

50–60 REINVENTING YOURSELF

60–75 A GENTLE DECLINE INTO SENILITY

75–85 YOUTH REGAINED

85–100 INHIBITIONS LOST. DON'T GIVE A DAMN. ME, ME, ME.

FORWARD

{Yes, I wrote my own Forward, which I learned
authors "don't do" but I did so sue me}

Not everyone believes they are creative. They think it's something only "special" people have. But the truth is, everyone is creative at something – the trick is finding out what.

Creativity is how we humans solve challenges in a positive way. And like sex, everyone can do it. Some are better at it. And when it's done well, it's AH-MAZING! Sex is a great metaphor to help convince you that you, too, are a celebrated, creative being with interesting solutions just queuing up to get out of your head – but only if you make the time to hear them shouting at you.

At the time of this writing, I am 46 years old. According to Paul Arden's "Life's Creative Circle"[1], I am in the beginning stages of "trying to keep up with the 25-year olds". OY!

Up until a few years ago, I played soccer on a women's team, on which most of the girls were in their 20s. There was no doubt they were agile, fit, fast and hungry. They ran circles around me on the field! Their skills and endurance kicked my booty. But the one thing I did have was 20 more years experience on the soccer field. I realized that although I could probably never outrun them to a ball, I could still play smart defense.

I learned that as long as I was patient, their inexperience would inevitably cause them to make an impulsive mistake. All I had to do was wait for it, and my opportunity to take the ball would naturally surface.

1 Paul Arden "It's not how Good you are, it's how Good you want to be", "Life's Creative Circle." (page 120)

In a business environment, we are all on the same team. What my soccer playing years taught me was to be patient with the 25 year olds. Yes, they are agile, hungry and fast. But they also will make rookie mistakes, and that's where a seasoned player can step in and teach them how to be a smarter player. Or a more patient player. Or whatever kind of player they could become to be a better player. Then we both learn how to be better – the coach, and the player.

I suggest to Mr. Arden that he augment his "Life's Creative Circle" for ages 45-50, to not come from a place of fear, but to come from a place of sharing what we know for the betterment of everyone. Maybe reword it to something like "Coaching the 25 year olds", or "Showing the 25 year olds what the old people know." Whatever the wording, you get the idea.

On this circle, I am also just four short years away from my 50th birthday, or "The Watershed." I didn't quite remember what "watershed" meant, so I consulted the Internet for the definition. Apparently, according to dictionary.com, I am very near to the stage in my life where I become a drainage area. #Maythewatersrunclearandmurkyinequalparts

But if you consider the second definition, it makes a lot of sense.

Creativity is like a river. Creativity, like a river, can be blocked; it can be dammed; it can rush and roar; and most importantly, it can flow. When creativity flows, you are being the very best expression of yourself, your ideas and your imagination.

But getting into the flow can be tricky.

It is definitely, harder than it looks. #TWSS

watershed

[**waw**-ter-shed, **wot**-er-] Spell Syllables

Examples   Word Origin

noun

1. *Chiefly British.* the ridge or crest line dividing two drainage areas;
    water parting; divide.

2. the region or area drained by a river, stream, etc.; drainage area.

3. *Architecture,* wash (def 44).

4. an important point of division or transition between two phases,
    conditions, etc.:
    *"The treaty to ban war in space may prove to be one of history's
    great watersheds."*

THE JEANS MY VERY LIFE DEPENDED ON

Gloria Vanderbilt

Amanda

IT'S HARDER THAN IT LOOKS

What is creativity anyway?

I've always loved making people laugh, and the process of drawing and writing. This is artistry, and artistry and creativity are sisters – related with the same DNA, but not at all the same. Not everyone is an artist. Not everyone loves to write or draw. But everyone has what's behind artistry, something that's way more important – imagination and curiosity.

My Dad has a Ph.D. in Economics, and he taught me a lot about how to be creative with managing my money from a young age. In 7th grade, I begged my parents for a pair of lavender Gloria Vanderbilt jeans (#childofthe80s), which cost about $60 in 1982.

They were SICK. I needed them. I loved them. My very existence depended on those purple jeans. Instead of buying them for me, my parents gave me a clothing allowance of $150 that I was free to spend any way I wanted. Wait… what?! You better believe buying a new pair of $60 jeans was off the table. I was forced to find a new solution. I went to a local consignment shop and found a used pair for $10, and came home with not just the jeans, but an entire bag full of used clothing! This lesson taught me really fast that I needed to get creative if I wanted something outside my reach.

Every single person in this world possesses imagination and curiosity… Which makes every human creative in their own way.

In my day job, I have the words "creative director" in my title. So people say to me all the time, "Oh, my God. You're so lucky you're creative. How do you do it?" I just look at them, and am like, "You are also creative. I don't care if you work at Home Depot, or you're an accountant, or you stay at home and take care of your kids. You are finding little ways every day to be creative, because the definition of creativity is taking things that haven't been together before and combining them to make something new."

OBLIGATORY STEVE JOBS QUOTE ->
CREATIVITY IS JUST CONNECTING THINGS. WHEN YOU ASK CREATIVE PEOPLE HOW THEY DID SOMETHING, THEY FEEL A LITTLE GUILTY BECAUSE THEY DIDN'T REALLY DO IT, THEY JUST SAW SOMETHING. IT SEEMED OBVIOUS TO THEM AFTER A WHILE. THAT'S BECAUSE THEY WERE ABLE TO CONNECT EXPERIENCES THEY'VE HAD AND SYNTHESIZE NEW THINGS.

We all have so much to learn from each other, and the only way to do that is to share what we've learned. Researching this book taught me A LOT. It really sparked my critical thinking about creativity, and as I was trying to figure out my own definition of what it meant to be creative, I started thinking about the word "creativity" itself.

Where did it come from? Who invented it? Why is it a thing?

The –ivity of it all

Creativity. Create –ivity. There are other words with this suffix –ivity. What do they mean? Product –ivity. Relat –ivity. Subject –ivity. Act –ivity. This got me curious.

It turns out the –ivity suffix meaning is way more complex than I'd imagined. J.L.Henshaw from Word's End explains it this way in his article from 2008[2]:

> The suffix "-ivity", has a fascinating complex meaning. It refers to improvement in the whole collection of related abilities of people, their knowledge and tools in applying to their environment for increasing the useful products they can produce. To understand labor "productivity", one also needs to understand the many related things that result in the total usefulness of tools, including things like a relaxing place to work so you can clear your mind between tasks...

> The suffix "-ivity" is shorthand for all that, in the case of "products". The same suffix is used similarly with the word "activity". There, "-ivity" contributes a similar shorthand for a complex physical system meaning for the case of "acts".

The article continues to explain.

> These words seem to be names for metaphors, culturally generated stand-ins for physical things, shaped to fit into the minds of people with the suitable personal and cultural values and links to prior discussions attached. They seem to be "value hubs" in the networks of meaning we construct our mental worlds from. My impression is that the correspondence or 'mapping' of the physical relationships that these metaphors serve to connect our personal and cultural values with is, by

comparison, disproportionately vague. That is to say, we pay a lot of attention to the internal meanings of language and relatively little to what any of it physically refers to.

Mr. Henshaw is quite the cunning linguist (Oh come on. I couldn't resist). But this is where you really puff puff pass.

Using Mr. Henshaw's observation and analysis, the concept of creativity refers little to the physical manifestation of the things created from it. It's referring to the connection to our personal, cultural and very human value attached to the act of creating *anything*.

In other words… it's the act of *doing it* that we desire.

In the beginning

We have been taught from the earliest texts that "creating" is the most sacred of actions. Since human kind has no scientific confirmation about where we really came from, we wonder and seek answers about who created us. Where do we come from? Genesis. Aliens. Who knows? My point is, that at the deepest level, we desire to understand creation, and are driven to create at all costs. It's the secret to happiness, the act of creating.

And when we're not in the constant pursuit toward our own individual expression of creating, we feel empty inside. We live in a state of dis-ease. We feel angry and purposeless.

This is why it seems harder than it looks. Because we haven't realized how deeply engrained this value is in our culture, and as a race, and haven't equipped ourselves with the teaching to help everyone understand. Those who feel they don't possess it observe being "creative" as an unobtainable gift. And most of those who exhibit creativity keep their process a dirty little secret, because it makes them feel special, validated and unique.

My advice? (BTW, I suck at remembering this, I should have these words tattooed on the insides of my eyeballs.)

Face your fears head on.

Constantly fight that voice in your head that says you can't do it, or you're not good enough. Everyone is creative, even if your kind of creative isn't for everyone. It's enough, if it's enough for you.

Your own version of creativity is needed here. The earth needs your energy, so give it all you've got – no matter how hard it looks.

But sometimes, you need a little stimulation.

SOMETIMES YOU NEED STIMULATION

Getting into the flow

Whenever I need to think critically about a new idea, I block off a 3-4 hour chunk of time in the afternoon when I can't be interrupted. Just me, my music and my laptop. I need that block of time to be uninterrupted, because I truly believe that when I set the right conditions for it, I can get into the zone and get everything done I need to get done, in whatever amount of time I have. In a way, it feels like I can distort time. It feels like everything around me in the world is happening on a normal timeline, but my space is somehow suspended in some strange wormhole.

Turns out, I'm not alone. This is called being in the "flow", and just like sex, when you're fully immersed in it, everything stops and speeds up at the same time. It's that magical place where the weight and worries of the world melt away and, for a brief time, the laws of the Universe are suspended.

I had the serendipitous opportunity to connect with Caroline Beaton, a researcher and writer for Psychology Today and Huffington Post. In the early stages of writing this book, I noticed that Caroline followed me on Twitter and her bio caught my attention, so I reached out to her in a DM (direct message). I rarely do this, but thought that she might know someone who could offer some actual science about creativity to balance my rhetoric. Caroline responded, and it turns out that she has focused most of her research on – yes, you guessed it – CREATIVITY. Holy she-at. #thankyouguides

She agreed to an interview with me, and man, is she a super smarty pants. "If you were doing a task that required 98% of your attention, like solving a math problem, you really wouldn't have the excess mental capacity to be creative," says Caroline. "Time specifically, is one of the main symptoms of flow, in that you lose track of it and you're completely absorbed in what you're doing. Un-creativity is actually learned… Flow is our natural state."

The nine tenets of "Getting into the Flow"

Mihaly Csikszentmihalyi is a positivity psychologist and author, most renowned for architecting the concept of the "flow" experienced during acts of creativity. (Because his last name has so many consecutive consonants and my mouth can't pronounce it, I will refer to him by his much shorter first name.)

Mihaly's concept of "flow" describes the feeling we humans experience when we're lost in a task that we care about so deeply that everything else – including our own sense of existence – melts away. Everyone has the ability to experience this; To paint a picture, think back about a time you had a really great orgasm. It's like that, but for your mind, and for hours.

In his incredible TED talk titled "Flow: The Secret to Happiness"[3], Mihaly explains that to understand what flow feels like, we have to understand what ecstasy is. "Ecstasy in Greek meant simply to 'stand to the side of something'," he says. "And then it became essentially an analogy for a mental state where you feel that you are not doing your ordinary everyday routines. So ecstasy is essentially a stepping into an alternative reality."

Can you imagine being in ecstasy for hours, every day? #Signmeupthankyou

According to Mihaly, there are nine components that must be present in order to achieve a "flow" state:

1. Challenge-skill balance

2. Merging of action and awareness

3. Clarity of goals

4. Immediate and unambiguous feedback

5. Concentration on the task at hand

6. Paradox of control

7. Transformation of time

8. Loss of self-consciousness

9. An autotelic experience

I had to look up "autotelic"; it means "Not motivated by anything beyond itself, thematically self-contained." In other words, doing it for love, not for anything else. #twss

Mihaly explains the connection between the nine flow conditions in this way. "There's this focus that, once it becomes intense, leads to a sense of ecstasy, a sense of clarity: you know exactly what you want to do from one moment to the other; you get immediate feedback. You know that what you need to do is possible to do, even though difficult, and sense of time disappears, you forget yourself, you feel part of something larger. And once the conditions are present, what you are doing becomes worth doing for its own sake."

About a year ago, I went to see this lady in Sonoma for a Reiki treatment (Reiki is energy healing, I highly recommend it, it's better than a massage and you feel unbelievable afterwards). I was telling her my frustration about not seeing any progress or movement with my first screenplay I had written, which at this time was about 3 years old (more

WHAT MAKES PEOPLE TRULY HAPPY –> "WHEN WE ARE INVOLVED IN CREATIVITY, WE FEEL THAT WE ARE LIVING MORE FULLY THAN DURING THE REST OF LIFE." ~ MIHALY CSIKSZENTMIHALYI

about this later). She asked me about the experience of writing it – how did it make me feel, what did I remember about those 9 months when I was writing it. I recalled to her how much joy it had brought me; the act of writing it felt so intense, that it felt like my eyes rolled back into my head and my fingers became the scribe of the players acting out the story in my head. That it felt like I wasn't actually writing it myself, but simply typing what was flowing through me as quickly as I could to not miss a single word.

She listened intently, and when I was finished she paused, and smiled at me and said, "and so it has done its job." <mic drop>

Mihaly also developed this cool model (if you know me, you know I love to build models! Super geeking out right now.) that guides you to how to achieve a flow state.

It basically says that if you want to get yourself there, both your skill level in whatever activity gets you off and how much of a challenge it is to do both have to be at their

Stimulation Checklist

☐ **Use clean sheets.**
Lots of blank ones. Scribble. Doodle. Draw Get every idea down on paper.

☐ **Do it outside.**
Listen to the streets. Smell the air. Feel the grass under your toes. Inspiration is all around us.

☐ **Juices.**
Put music on. Light candles. Get salty snacks and beer. Toys. Games. Crayons. Whatever gets them going! Unleash your inner kid and remember what it's like to set your mind free.

Csíkszentmihályi's Flow

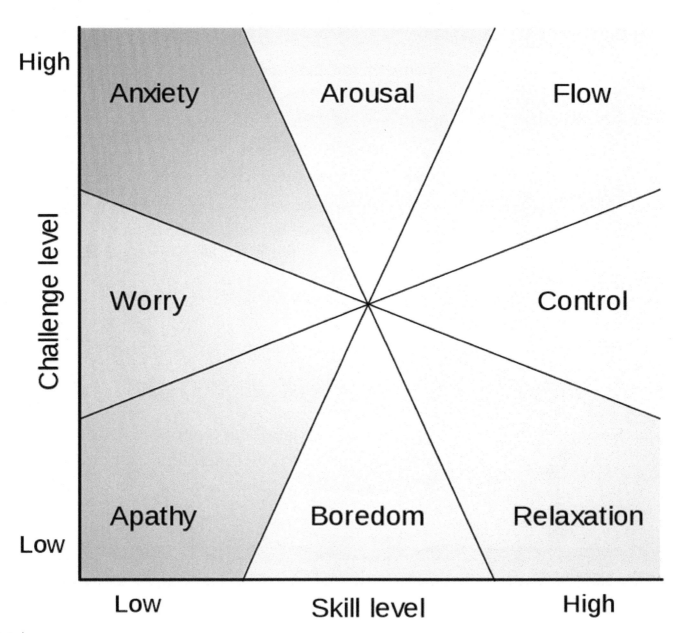

highest level. If they're not, you just end up bored, frustrated, and not caring about it.

This model can also be applied to relationships, which I believe are living, breathing organisms themselves. You have to study and monitor them constantly, understand how their individual cells are morphing, how the environment is affecting it, and what transitional state it's in at the moment. They are fragile and strong at the same time.

The only way to keep them thriving is to keep things interesting, which can be an ongoing challenge, unless you're open to Reason #3: Turn yourself upside down.

TURN YOURSELF UPSIDE DOWN

Being square makes it easier

Do you remember those old activity books sold in airport gift shops, the kind with the invisible ink pen and other fun brain teasers designed to keep a kid busy enough for a 2-hour flight? I LOVED those things. One of the puzzles was recreating a drawing by using a grid system, so instead of your eye trying to draw the entire image at once, it forces you to only look at one small, nondescript square at a time.

Doing this turns each square into a series of lines and shapes, removing the meaning of what the image represents to you. Detaching personal meaning about the bigger picture removes the brain's ability to morph how it looks to you, which can easily distort your interpretation of how the placement of the lines and shapes should appear on the paper. When you focus only on the smaller squares, you end up drawing the bigger picture pretty damn well.

Looking at things in a different way breaks your brain.

When it comes to artistry, or even problem solving, breaking down a larger challenge into smaller chunks is a great example of making small strides that can benefit the greater outcome. It makes the tasks less overwhelming, which can prevent shutting down the brain's receptiveness to keep going.

I know for me writing this book, I needed to tackle a chapter a week – and only one specific chapter a week – otherwise I found myself scattered and all over the place, feeling like there would never be an end.

Mash it up

"What Would I Say?" is an application that automatically generates new Facebook posts out of portions of posts you actually made. Per their website[4], "…it trains a Markov Bot based on mixture model of bigram and unigram probabilities derived from your past post history. The results are often hilarious – it all depends on what you've written on Facebook."

Oookkeeee… I don't know what a bigram or unigram is, but I do know mixing up my words to make nonsense is funny! These could all be punchlines to jokes I seriously want to hear.

Here are a few of my favorite #WWIS combinations from my own Facebook statuses ->

Weird, useless and awesome, right?! #Distractedfordays

Open yourself up to playing with someone else

Here's another fun way to make your synapses connect with new neural friends inside your brain. I recently played a social media game called #MyFiveWordRomanceNovel where players are challenged to come up with a five word sentence that describes a romantic (or otherwise raunchy or adult) story.

My friend Matt Ridings and I spent the better part of an afternoon in a #MyFiveWordRomanceNovel smackdown. Yes, I was immensely entertained.

Dick Long white beard and a few hours for only $180!?
— ME

Fell behind the pan flute salute. Hmm.
— ME

Yes, it just grows down... so...
— ME

Just made a strange beeping in there...
— ME

Please vote for clarity.
— ME

Omg business people.
— ME

Courtney Smith Kramer Is this supposed to itch? #CollegeVersion
#MyFiveWordRomanceNovel

Like · Reply · 16 hrs

∧ Hide 19 Replies

 Matt Ridings Hand sanitizer doesn't go there.
#MyFiveWordRomanceNovel

Like · Reply · 16 hrs

Courtney Smith Kramer Yup, burns too damn badly
#MyFiveWordRomanceNovel

Like · Reply · 16 hrs

Matt Ridings Penicillin is like genital magic
#MyFiveWordRomanceNovel

Like · Reply · 16 hrs

Courtney Smith Kramer Magic genitals have sparkly wands
#MyFiveWordRomanceNovel

Like · Reply · 16 hrs

Matt Ridings That is not a wand. #MyFiveWordRomanceNovel

Like · Reply · 16 hrs

Courtney Smith Kramer What is shooting out then?
#MyFiveWordRomanceNovel

Like · Reply · 16 hrs

Matt Ridings Hogwarts are on my Dumbledore.
#MyFiveWordRomanceNovel

Like · Reply · 16 hrs

Courtney Smith Kramer Better than Slitheryn on Hufflepuff.
#MyFiveWordRomanceNovel

Like · Reply · 16 hrs

Matt Ridings Slitheryn....that's what she said.
#MyFiveWordRomanceNovel

Like · Reply · 16 hrs

Courtney Smith Kramer Hufflepuff... that's what Bruce said.
#MyFiveWordRomanceNovel
Like · Reply · 16 hrs

Matt Ridings Have change for a twenty? #LowEndHufflePuff
#MyFiveWordRomanceNovel
Like · Reply · 16 hrs

Matt Ridings Will there be salad tossing?
#MyFiveWordRomanceNovel #PrisonVersion
Like · Reply · 16 hrs

Courtney Smith Kramer Fencing is more my style.
#MyFiveWordRomanceNovel
Like · Reply · 16 hrs

Matt Ridings I don't do sword fights. #MyFiveWordRomanceNovel
Like · Reply · 16 hrs

Courtney Smith Kramer My sword is very large
#MyFiveWordRomanceNovel
Like · Reply · 16 hrs

Matt Ridings My hands are normal size.
#MyFiveWordRomanceNovel #TrumpVersion
Like · Reply · 16 hrs

Courtney Smith Kramer I was thinking your mouth.
#MyFiveWordRomanceNovel
Like · Reply · 16 hrs

Matt Ridings Sorry, I just got distracted. #MyFiveWordRomanceNovel
Unlike · Reply · 👍 1 · 16 hrs

Courtney Smith Kramer Happens to us all, friend.
#MyFiveWordRomanceNovel
Like · Reply · 15 hrs

Being playful, game play and doing stuff just for the sheer joy of it is so necessary in our serious lives. God knows there's enough awful news, people and situations out there to last us a lifetime of tears. So you chose what you let in – and as much as I can, playfulness gets a VIP pass in my line.

Study others closely

I am a total science nerd. I'm fascinated by quantum theories, energy, universal explanations and connections we can't see or explain. When it comes to sparking creativity, sometimes it's cool to study the work of others who you admire to make you critically think about subjects you might not normally ponder on a daily basis.

Nikoli Tesla is one of the greatest geniuses of all time. The way his mind organized numbers and organic fractals together is so simple yet simply mind-blowing. Here's an example of his "Map to Multiplication", which showed that if you position numbers on a spiral matrix, not only does it align to their multipliers, but also connects together all numbers in a fractal-edged series of shapes within this spiral.

I also find it an interesting inside message that he was possibly trying to communicate in dating this piece of work "12/12/12". The number 12 has significance in numerous spiritual contexts, being said to represent the governance of the cosmos, having 12 signs of the zodiac, as well as signifying authority, appointment and completeness. It is also said to signify God, being double that of the numbers said to represent the Devil – 666.

In numerology, it means "Charismatic, self-reliant, fun-lover, good singer"#WTF?

Please do make sure the next time we go karaoke-ing, choose for me the 12th song on page 12. I'll sing it no matter what!

N. TESLA
MAP TO MULTIPLICATION

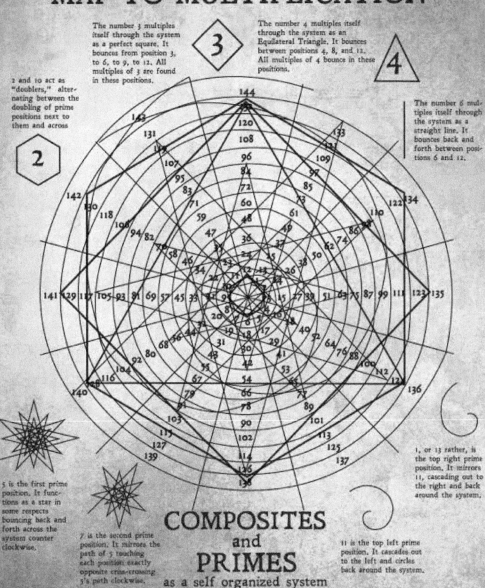

The number 3 multiples itself through the system as a perfect square. It bounces from position 3, to 6, to 9, to 12. All multiples of 3 are found in these positions.

3

The number 4 multiples itself through the system as an Equilateral Triangle. It bounces between positions 4, 8, and 12. All multiples of 4 bounce in these positions.

4

2 and 10 act as "doublers," alternating between the doubling of prime positions next to them and across

2

The number 6 multiples itself through the system as a straight line. It bounces back and forth between positions 6 and 12.

5 is the first prime position. It functions as a star in some respects bouncing back and forth across the system counter clockwise.

7 is the second prime position. It mirrors the path of 5 touching each position exactly opposite criss-crossing 5's path clockwise.

1, or 13 rather, is the top right prime position. It mirrors 11, cascading out to the right and back around the system.

11 is the top left prime position. It cascades out to the left and circles back around the system.

COMPOSITES
and
PRIMES
as a self organized system

Exceptions to the prime positions occur when primes interact with each other. The first exception (25) to the prime position is when 5 multiples by itself, or is squared. The second exception (35) is 5 interacting with 7. All other exceptions are multiples of 5 and 7 or 11 and 13. All squared primes land in position 1. All twin primes (pairs on the sides of 6 or 12 add up to be a multiple of 12.

Nikola Tesla Inventor

When *not* to turn yourself upside down

While turning your brain cells upside down is a good thing to inspire creativity, turning your physical body upside down during sex is not a good idea at all. In fact, according the website "The Frisky", 6 of the 10 most dangerous sexual positions involve one or more partners in the upside down position[5]. It turns out that our elbow and knee joints are simply not made to be uber load-bearing points, and if you decide to try any of these positions, do so at your own risk.

What I have found from experience, is if you spend more time thinking about your balance than you do the act of what's putting you in that position in the first place, it's probably best to choose a different way to do it. #howdyougetthatblackeye?

Since those "Joy of Sex" illustrations are just weird (and side note, would it have killed them to buy a razor?! #whyistherehairthere #justsayin), here are my rough stick drawings to show you what they are. Fair warning… you can never unsee these.

TOP 10 MOST DANGEROUS SEXUAL POSITIONS

1. THE PICK ME UP

2. PAIR OF TONGS

3. FIRE HYDRANT

4. THE HEAD SPINNER

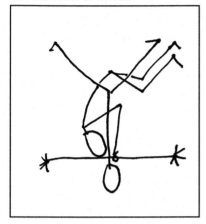

5. BUMPER CARS

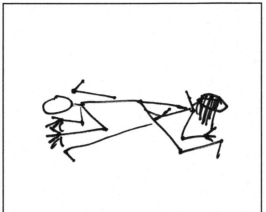

6. TRIPLE LINDY

7. THE WHEELBARROW

8. THE BACK BREAKER

9. LONDON BRIDGE

10. THE POGO STICK

YOU CAN DO IT SOLO, BUT IT'S BETTER WITH OTHERS

Do it together

"We humans are a mass of contradictions,"[6] says Andre Walton, visiting professor of creativity and entrepreneurship at the University of South Wales and author of *Embracing the New Era: Managing oneself and others into the era of creativity.*

"When we're group-oriented, enjoying the safety and sense of companionship that group membership provides, it is our similarity to others that is salient," Walton says. "And when we're indulging in our need for individuality, enjoying a sense of uniqueness, it's our dissimilarity from others that is critical."

I want to be exactly like you but totally different.

Walton's research shows that it's the dissimilar condition that draws the more unique, creative connections in our brain. Yet our intense need to connect with other humans in groups works counter-intuitively against this tendency, creating almost a "creativity-killer" scenario. He found that when humans experience times of grief or stress, for instance, we tend to cluster together in groups, and creativity is suppressed.

So why do we start with group brainstorming as a way to elicit creative ideas? This activity was popularized by advertising executive Alex Osborn in his 1953 book *Applied*

Imagination as a way to produce a higher volume of ideas around a topic. But research has shown that the exact opposite is true. It turns out that people need time as an individual to formulate ideas before coming together as a group to discuss them.

"Collaboration is a tricky one. Research has found that face-to-face collaboration can shut down creativity, because people get nervous and scared about how people will perceive them, and that elevates the analytical side of their brain, which subdues the creative, spontaneous side of their brain," says Caroline Beaton. "The one thing research has found that's really effective is written collaboration. So, for example, you could be texting ideas back and forth with a group where you are essentially allowed to be alone, but can still ping pong ideas back and forth without being scared that you're going to be shut down. I think that when people feel like they're put on the spot, they tend to be less creative because all of these other forces intervene like, 'How am I going to be perceived?' And if you're thinking about how you're going to be perceived, then it's really hard to create any unique, original content."

FACE TO FACE COLLABORATION CAN SHUT DOWN CREATIVITY, BECAUSE PEOPLE GET NERVOUS AND SCARED ABOUT HOW PEOPLE WILL PERCEIVE THEM.

This approach is supported further in research led by psychologist Paul Paulus, PhD, of the University of Texas at Arlington, who points to the surprising effectiveness of group "brainwriting," in which group members write their ideas on paper and pass them to others in the group, who then add their own ideas to the list. In a 2000 Organizational Behavior and Human

Decision Processes (Vol. 82, No. 1) study led by Paulus, an interactive group of brainwriters produced 28 percent more possible uses for a paper clip than a similar group of solitary brainwriters.

Hallelujah! I was just saying to myself that I am in need of 28% more uses for a paper clip in my life. No seriously. Search for "Binder Clip Hacks" on YouTube and prepare to be amazed. #cliphacks

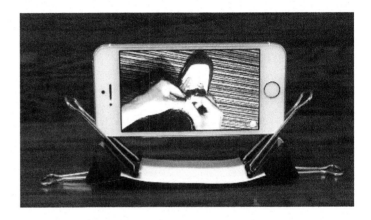

It seems the consensus, with Walton, Beaton and Paulus, that the old adage "there are no bad ideas in brainstorming" is completely false. It's just the brave ones who are unafraid of being judged by their peers who share them out loud.

When it feels good to do it alone

I am an introvert, which surprises a lot of people. What this means to me, is in order to recharge my batteries, I need alone time and quiet. Crowds literally suck the life out of me, so this alone time is necessary – especially in my own creative ideation process.

As exciting as it is to form new and interesting ideas through collaboration, when we work alone, it's refreshing to have the space to explore our own minds, perhaps connecting new thoughts from within that can spark something exciting.

I wholeheartedly agree that there's a time and a place for alone time *and* group sharing of ideas. I personally have found that group collaboration is great for sparking new strains and tangents of thinking that create more robust ideas. I never thought I was the type of person to "need time to think", but the older I get, the more I realize it does take me more time to process information and come to a solution I can really stand behind.

Are my standards just higher now? Meh. It's probably all the wine.

Being a flow-n ranger

When you're working "alone"… are you? We have access to information online, in books, and many reference materials that help us inform our own narrative. But more importantly, when we get into the flow, there's no stopping the voices that are dying to break through.

George Lucas gave a great podcast interview about his approach to writing screenplays, where he comments, "There comes a point where the characters are narrating themselves, and even if I wanted to write something different, they won't let me. They take on a life of their own, and I am simply recording what they're saying and doing." #DyingtochannelthevoicesinGeorgeLucas'head

The multiple and spontaneous ones

If I say the name "Elisha Gray", would you guess that this person is 1) a new character on a Shonda Rhimes show 2) a billionaire obsessed with S&M 3) a new backup dancer for Beyonce´ or 4) the original inventor of the telephone.

As much as I want to explore 1) through 3), the answer is 4).

On the morning of February 14, 1876, Ohio-born engineer Elisha Gray filed a patent for his "acoustic telegraph" at the U.S. Patent office, just hours before Alexander Graham

~ IDIOM TRANSLATOR ~

SOMETIMES, WHAT PEOPLE SAY ISN'T WHAT THEY *REALLY* MEAN. HERE IS A TRANSLATION:

"I WANT TO BOUNCE AN IDEA OFF YOU" *REALLY MEANS* "I NEED YOU TO VALIDATE THAT I AM AS BRILLIANT AS I THINK I AM."

"I WANT TO PICK YOUR BRAIN" *REALLY MEANS* "I HAVE NO CLUE WHAT I AM DOING AND NEED IDEAS FROM YOU FOR FREE."

"LET'S PUT THAT IDEA IN OUR BACK POCKET" *REALLY MEANS* "I HAVE NEVER HEARD ANYTHING SO STUPID IN MY LIFE, DON'T EVER SPEAK OF IT AGAIN."

Bell, a Scottish-born engineer in Boston, filed his very similar patent at the same office via his lawyer in Washington DC[7].

The controversy surrounding the intense fight that ensued over the next 12 years is mired in drama; accusations of scandal, bribery, deceit and theft. It is said that when Bell's attorney delivered the patent to the US Patent office, he caught a glimpse of Gray's patent and realizing it was similar, bribed the clerk to list his as being received first. After years of litigation, it was ruled that although Gray was the first to successfully test the device known now as a telephone, Bell was the first to write the invention down and was therefore declared the official inventor. #dude

(Derek Waters' show "Drunk History" does an incredibly funnier depiction of this story, I beg you to go watch it on YouTube, like now.)

Gray did go on to invent the early fax machine and praise God, the electric synthesizer (the 80s thank you!). FUN FACT: During the testing period of his telephone invention, Bell hired a young protégé named Thomas Watson, now famous for founding a company called International Business Systems, or IBM.

The first words muttered through Bell's telephone were "Mr. Watson, come here, I want to see you" – not in reference to a more well-known Mr. Watson who we know from Sherlock Holmes, but to his assistant, Tom. Perhaps the former would have been a better choice, considering the mysterious circumstances that gave Alexander his now infamous place in history?!

Despite the crazy circumstances surrounding this story, the bigger picture craziness is that all things being equal – access to information, education, money, tools and resources

- what could explain its simultaneous discovery and the filing of the patents within just a few hours of each other?

Although there is no hard scientific explanation as to why ideas sharing common themes seem to surface at the same time, it is officially described as "Multiple Discovery Theory", or simultaneous invention.

We all know that multiple and simultaneous of anything is a good thing.

But in this case, it helps explain what happens when our human brains synthesize a common set of patterns set forth culturally, scientifically, artistically, etcetera, etcetera - meaning all the inputs of life work together in certain ways to contribute to pockets of study that start to form patterns, that are then filtered and analyzed through our human brains, which have also been influenced by input patterns in our environment, education and upbringing, which allow the possibilities of similar ideas happening at the same time. #takeabreath

Our human brains can only synthesize information within a certain range and rate, causing the probability of these similar ideas to happen roughly in the same time frame.

Going deeper #twss, the theory of "recombinant paradigms"[8] hypothesizes that the recurrence of patterns yielding similar bodies of work serve to validate our scientific findings and civility as a society. "I feel valid and civil!" said no pattern ever.

Now they lost me. Who would like a simpler answer, raise your hand! Brought to you in the form of another #puffpuffpass moment: I personally believe that thoughts are things, and when they're released into the ether we don't yet understand, they become part of our collective energy flow, ready for the taking by anyone able and open to receive

7 https://en.wikipedia.org/wiki/Alexander_Graham_Bell
8 https://en.wikipedia.org/wiki/Multiple_discovery

them. I believe that when Multiple Discoveries occur, it's just a validation that it's time for that idea or invention to be a part of our collective story. May the person currently writing my exact same book right now be damned, a thousand plagues onto your house and I mean that in the nicest possible way.

When you want to do it with lots of others

Apparently in Japan, they REALLY prefer to do it with others. According to the website Oddee,[9] "Japan has successfully set a new world record – having 250 men and 250 women consent to have sex in the same place at the same time, completing the world's biggest orgy. The Orgy was held in a warehouse with a professional camera crew taking pictures and recording the entire event. Each sex act and position was choreographed so that couples were simultaneous in their actions.'

Despite the "orgy" label, the 250 couples (all tested STD-free and presumably sponsored by Kleenex®) featured in the video have sex only with each other and not with any other couple. The entire event is available for purchase on DVD.

There's a sushi joke in there somewhere. #nowords

9 http://www.oddee.com/item_97082.aspx

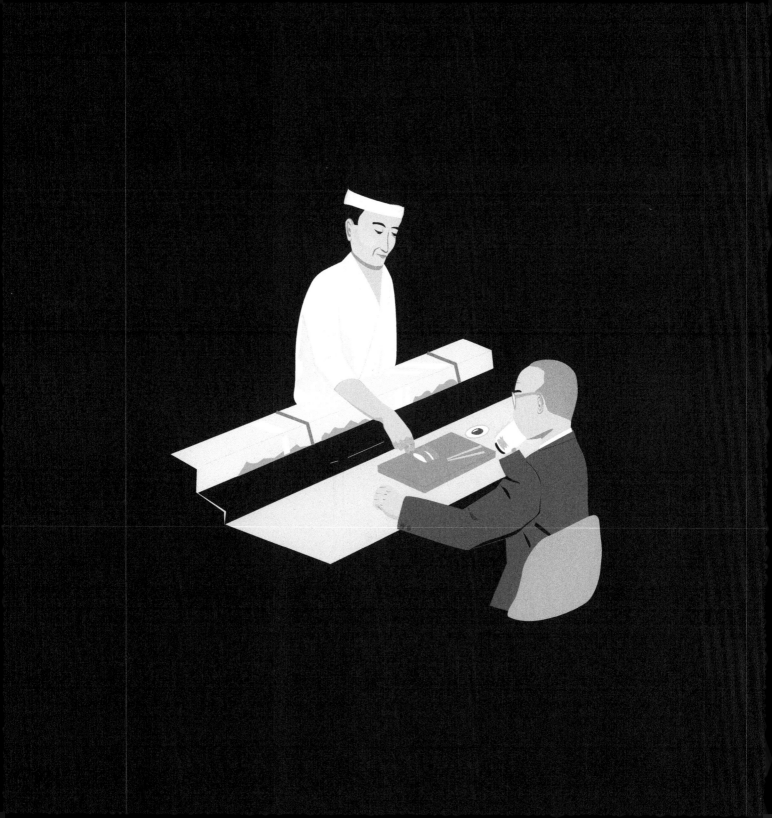

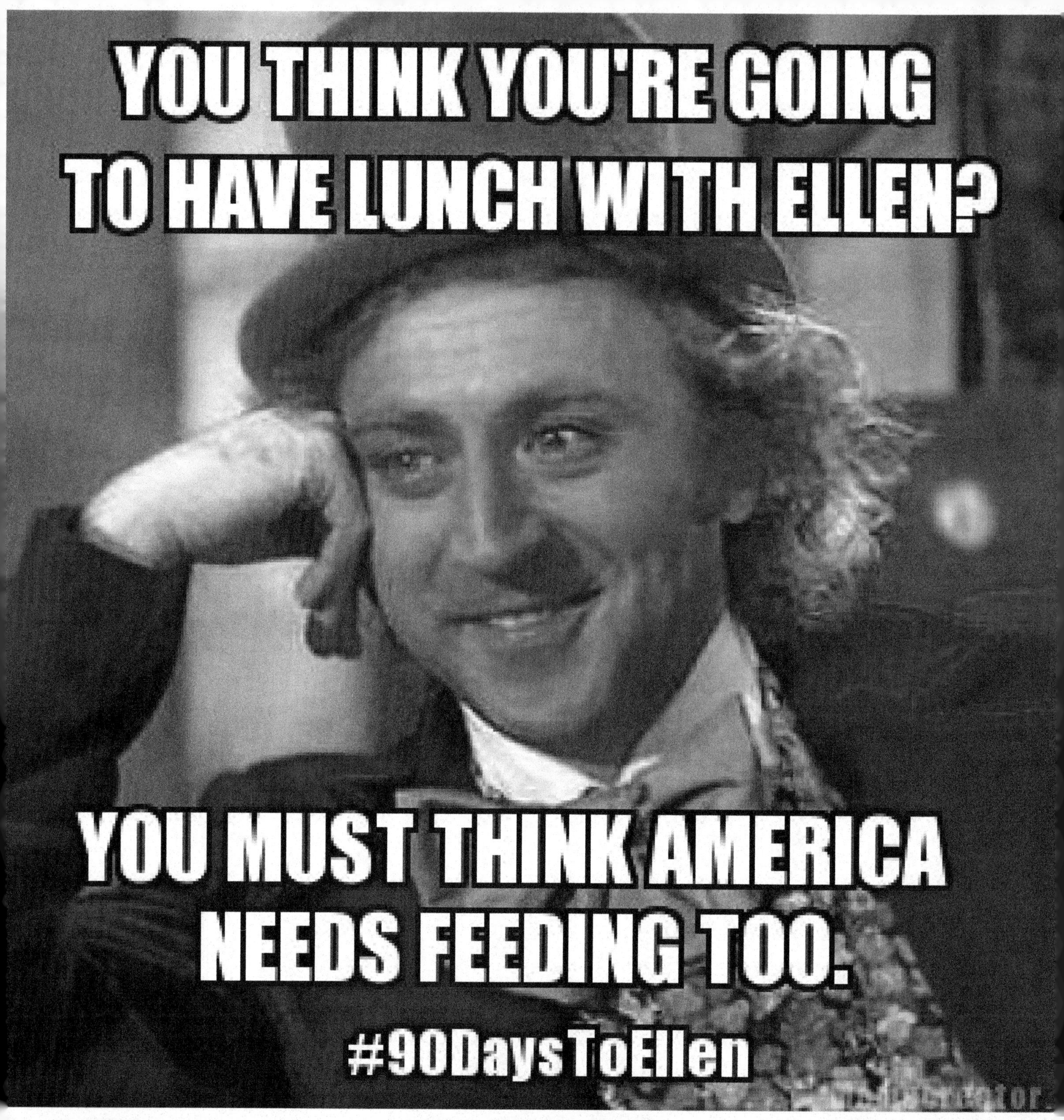
YOU THINK YOU'RE GOING
TO HAVE LUNCH WITH ELLEN?
YOU MUST THINK AMERICA
NEEDS FEEDING TOO.
#90DaysToEllen

RELINQUISH CONTROL

Knowing when to let others take the lead

Oooh la la, nothing says get your sexy on like handing the reins over to someone else, would you agree Mr. Grey (this time not referring to the one who got screwed by the telephone patent.)? The same is true for creativity when it comes to letting a trusted community help shape the way a campaign builds itself out. (Campaign in this reference means any idea a group is collectively trying to make happen, together.)

When it comes to creativity, letting go of ownership of the flow of a campaign is a secret solution for success and community participation. It unlocks the door for new creativity by a community, because no one person can have all the creative solutions for a campaign. In Improv comedy, the number one rule is never using the word "No." When your partner pitches an idea to you, you're required to build upon it with a "Yes, AND" which makes it keep going. Applying this rule of Improv is a great and reliable way to include your community in helping to shape the narrative of a campaign, while building interest, engagement and shareability. #buzzwordalert

We first tested out this theory a few summers ago when Bryan, our friend DJ Waldow, his wife Kristina and I ran our "90 Days to Ellen"[10] social campaign experiment. Our premise was simple: To prove that anyone could use social media to meet anyone, even a celebrity. We tried to think it through as best as we could, and devised our plan to only use social media to entice Ellen DeGeneres to have lunch with Bryan and DJ. We thought that if we could get national food establishments to "outbid" each other with donations to the awesome charity *Feeding America,* in an effort to win the chance to host the lunch, if Ellen ever agreed, it was a win/win for everyone. We made it clear that this was not a ploy to get on the show; in fact, we wanted the lunch to be a private experience for the winning food establishment and Bryan and DJ. Our plan seemed fool proof. What could possibly go wrong?

For 90 days, we Tweeted, Facebooked, Vined and Instagrammed our faces off trying to get someone from the Ellen Degeneres show to acknowledge, engage, and agree to the lunch. We wrote blog posts, and encouraged people following the #90DaystoEllen hashtag to share their ideas for the efforts. We watched as our community snowballed in size, cheerleading our efforts in real time in hopes the experiment would work.

Applebee's reached out to us, as they'd been watching the campaign and explained that they couldn't donate any money but instead sent us a set of 6 "Lunch Decoys" (basically life-sized blow up dolls) to use as we wanted. One of these dolls looked like Ellen, and she became our official mascot toward the end of the 90 days. Buzz continued to build about the campaign, and articles were written about it in Advertising Age and Forbes.

As Day 90 came to a close, and the timer ticked its way down to zero, our community of thousands watched with bated breath. We had gotten as far up the chain as exchanging emails with her Executive Producer, who at the 11th hour gave us a resounding, "Not interested." NOOOOOOOOOOOOOOOOOOOOOO!!

To say we were disappointed is an understatement. But in reflection, it turns out that we were the real winners. We learned a hell of a lot about community building, social interaction, and campaign planning. 90 Days to Ellen was not a failure. We raised $1,500 for Feeding America, thanks to the International Culinary Center. We earned over 150 million social impressions on Twitter alone (which had we paid for those impressions using Twitter's $8 cost per thousand, it would have cost us $1.2 million dollars!). And most importantly, we made tons of new social friends who, by their own volition and creativity, took the campaign to new levels because we just said "Yes, and…". Not bad for the less than $25 we spent on the campaign.

It was the most fun and exhausting 90 days in my campaign career. The experience almost killed me, but damn does it make for a great story - something I'd be willing to do just about anything for. To this day, we still have no idea if Ellen even knew that this was happening. I sense that someday we will find out though, at which point we will either receive a hearty laugh from her, or a restraining order. #5050chance

Make it rain

Many of you may remember the ALS "Ice Bucket Challenge" fundraising campaign from the summer of 2015. The campaign went like this:

1. Make a video of you calling out three friends to join the challenge to raise money for ALS (also known as Lou Gehrig's Disease) research by the ALS Association

2. Dump ice cold water over your head

3. Share the video and donate money yourself

It is rumored to have been started by former Boston College baseball player Pete Frates, who was diagnosed with the disease in 2011. In early summer 2015, he videoed himself dumping ice water over his head, and challenged a few of his NFL and celebrity buddies to "strike out ALS". That's all it took to go viral.

It was so fun to be publicly challenged on video by a friend to take part. The videos over time got more and more creative, including morphing away from just individuals into entire NFL teams challenging other teams to participate together. Celebrities like Charlie Sheen and Jennifer Lopez made their own personal videos, making them seem "just like us" for a minute, at least. According to Wikipedia, the campaign raised over $100 million for the ALS Association and just recently, reported that this money helped researchers *find a cure* for ALS. #wow

What's interesting in studying this effort, and taking what we learned from our 90 Days to Ellen experiment, a pattern emerged. Bryan touched upon this in his first book, but it continues to be why we believe it's the secret to what makes a campaign go viral, because it's proven again and again.

We call it, "The Secret to Making Campaigns Go Viral":

1. Keep the premise simple (and fun, a bonus!)

2. Make it easy to share

3. Get it to a social catalyst early on who already cares about you or your cause

4. Apply the rules of Improv – "Yes, and…"

Understanding this, and looking for it in other successful campaigns has definitely influenced our own approach in how we craft our client campaigns. The IBM #NewWayToWork Influencer program was filtered through these tenets. At the time of this writing, the #NewWayToWork hashtag had earned over three Billion – yes, **Billion** with a B – Twitter impressions in just over a year.

The content and experiences we created together with IBM and our "Futurists" Influencers were educational, simple and fun, and easy to share, which helped us forge lasting relationships with everyone involved.

Here's a cool story about how both 90 Days and the ALS challenge came together for me on a personal level. Wanting to have some fun, Bryan and I made a video for the Ice Bucket Challenge that implicated our dog, Jessie, as the dumper of the ice. We posted the video and shared it, and a few days later got a Tweet from Jon

Steiert, a friend we had met online during our 90 Days to Ellen campaign, sharing that he had featured our video and Jessie on Pet360.com where he worked at the time. What a happy surprise! This serendipitous interaction never would have happened without a whole bunch of people just saying "Who the eff cares? Bring it!"

Note to self: Daily mantra -> "Who the eff cares? Bring it!"

What about relinquishing control and sex?

Relinquishing control in the form of letting down your inhibitions with someone you trust can be a very erotic and exciting activity. From simply flirting on one side, to the extreme of role-playing and BDSM (Bondage/Discipline/Sadism/Masochism), there lies a full range of the extent one could take to let someone else drive.

According to Wikipedia, "Unlike the usual 'power neutral' relationships and play styles commonly followed by couples, activities and relationships, within a BDSM context are often characterized by the participants' taking on complementary, but unequal roles; thus, the idea of informed consent of both the partners becomes essential. Participants who exert sexual dominance over their partners are known as dominants or tops, while participants who take the passive, receiving, or obedient role are known as submissives or bottoms."[11]

Until I was researching this book, "tops" and "bottoms" were something I searched for at Nordstrom Rack. Obligatory public safety message: How far you and your partner want to venture into relinquishing control, talking about and establishing shared consent and boundaries is essential to a safe experience.

11 https://en.wikipedia.org/wiki/BDSM

EVERYONE WANTS TO BE A PART OF SOMETHING BIGGER THAN THEMSELVES. #TWSS

Start with wordplay

Mutual consent is also necessary for dirty talk and sexting, an activity that according to Tina Horn in her book *Sexting: The Grownup's Little Book of Sex Tips for Getting Dirty Digitally*[12], is a "...powerful tool and an exciting toy for generating attraction and connection between people."

She offers some simple wordplay formulas to get your sexting "A" game going. After using some of these, I am sure the only thing you'll wish for is more fingers:

Compliment: *I really love the way you [verb] your [anatomy] all over my [anatomy].*

Asking for what you want: *Please [verb] my [anatomy] like you did last night.*

Hyperbolic Compliment: *That was the best [noun] I've ever had!*

Guidance: *If you keep [verb]ing like that, I'm gonna [verb] so [adjective].*

Identity: *Yeah you like it when I [activity] you, don't you, you little [identity]?*

Order: *I want you to come over and [verb] your [adjective], [adjective] [noun] on my [anatomy].*

Praise: *You look so [adjective] tonight, it makes me wanna [verb] you all over.*

Seduction: *I'm going to [verb] you and [verb] you until you [verb].*

Domination and Submission: *Please may I have permission to [verb] your [noun], [honorarium]?*

And for my heterosexual male readers, some sound advice: You might want to stick to just using words, at least half of the time.

Glamour Magazine[13] polled 1000 heterosexual women and, when asked if they wanted their dream guy to send them X-rated pictures, 46% said "No way, no one wants to see that."

Finally quantified: The pen is officially 54% mightier than the sword.

12 orn, Tina (2015-12-15). Sexting: The Grownup's Little Book of Sex Tips for Getting Dirty Digitally (Kindle Locations 355-359). Quiver Books
13 February 2016 Glamour Magazine, page 102

THE MORE YOU HAVE, THE BETTER YOU FEEL

The importance of quantity, quality and endurance

When it comes to creativity and ideas, it really is about quality, quantity and endurance. The more ideas that are thrown onto the table, the easier it is to choose the really, really good ones from the completely terrible ones.

I came across an article that said there are scientific facts to support the physiological reasons why we're hardwired to be better at doing some things at certain times of the day. The author writes, "We know that the creative mind is an early riser and that the editing mind sleeps in," rationalizing that the prefrontal cortex is most active immediately after waking, and ones willpower to write is most logically in the morning before it's worn down by the stressors of the day like work, kids, chores, etc.

I'm calling bullshit on this.

Creativity is about connections. Whatever time of the day works for you, your process, and the problem you're trying to solve is what's right for you. Although scientifically it may be true that the brain is hardwired to fire faster or in different ways when you first wake up, I don't believe that's the only factor that goes into producing really creative ideas. What is important is that you consciously create the conditions you need to allow for the non-linear connections in your brain to find each other – which can be created at any time of the day or night.

"Creativity does have that same building effect that sex does," explains Caroline Beaton. "So not only the more ideas you have, the more you are creative, but actually the content of your creative thought becomes improved, because you're actually increasing connections in your brain surrounding a certain topic. The more neurons that are firing together around a certain thing or subject, passion, endeavor, the more you're going to create those connections, the more complex they're going to be, and then ultimately the better your work will be."

I can tell you that, at least for me, I required a LOT of writing endurance to finish this baby you're reading right now. It's kinda like how I imagine a runner feels ; you put it off but know you have to do it, it's painful to get started, but after you get going it's kinda fun, and when you hit your stride you're optimistic, happy and on top of the world. Then, when you finish, you feel a sense of accomplishment and honor for yourself for completing the run!

But then you realize you need to do it again – another 20 times – and you pour yourself a glass of wine and turn on bad reality TV so you don't have to think about it.

#FML. But I love it. And hate it. But love it.

Look at the models

Ryan Campbell, a super smart marketing colleague of mine, is the king of model building (and they're mostly brown – his favorite color). There aren't enough circles and squares left in Powerpoint to build more models than we've built together. Models are a great tool to give structure and boundaries around the problem you're trying to solve… but do they really make you more creative?

We've found the best use for models in the creative process is to provide a way to organize your ideas in a way that makes it easier to assess and objectify things that are inherently subjective. When it comes to business, there is never enough time in a presentation to provide all the back thinking and strategy that goes into arriving to a really great idea. By providing context around the creative ideas through a model, it helps an audience better understand what an idea could mean in a particular

MODELS HELP PRIORITIZE AND CONTEXTUALIZE OUR IDEAS SO WE KNOW WHAT WE'RE GETTING INTO.

situation (under the parameters of budget, level of effort, time, resources necessary to execute it, etc.), instead of in a vacuum out of context.

Experimentation is encouraged

How do you generate a lot of ideas? Tom Kelly, one of the founders of global design and innovation firm IDEO and creativity expert himself, made up his own reason why creativity is like sex without even knowing it: "The more you do it, the easier it gets."[14]

Of course, he's referencing the practice of creativity, and offers up three techniques to get the ideas flowing: Mind Mapping, 30 Circles, and Empathy Maps. Each of these techniques offers a structure to help push divergent thinking – a thought process or method used to generate creative ideas by exploring many possible solutions.

14 https://hbr.org/2013/11/three-creativity-challenges-from-ideos-leaders&cm_sp=Article-_-Links-_-End%20of%20Page%20Recirculation

MINDMAPPING

Start with your challenge in the center and surround it by various possibilities. Then play out each scenario to think through different ways to solve it.

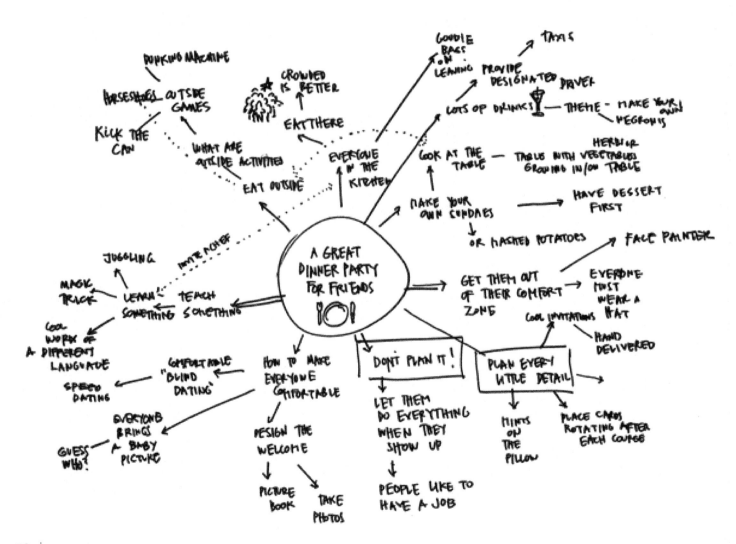

30 CIRCLES

Start with 30 blank circles and transform them all in 2 minutes or less. This one was created by Tim Brown, CEO of IDEO, in a TED session. (Can you tell I love this company?!)

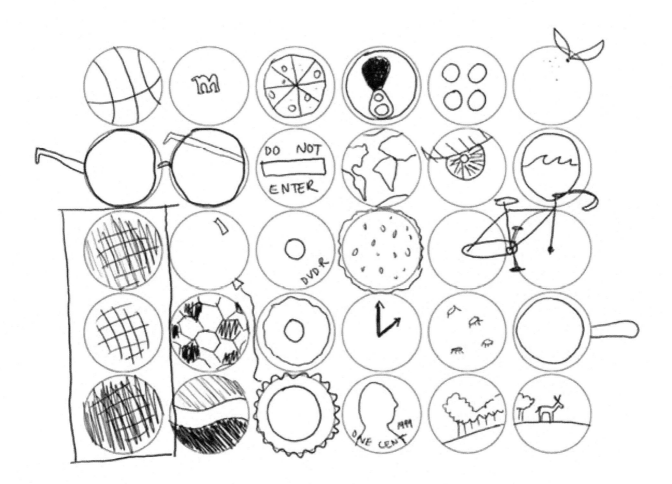

EMPATHY MAP

Fill out each quadrant with how the challenge you're trying to solve might feel, think, do and say. This puts you inside the challenge to understand it better instead of generalizing a solution and is a part of "Design Thinking".

Do it at the last minute

Organizational psychologist Adam Grant gave an incredible TED talk called "The surprising habits of original thinkers"[15]. In the talk, he is intrigued by the idea that precrastinators – not a typo, it's the opposite of procrastination, something we all can identify with – had to be "more creative" in the ideas they created because of the amount of time they spent preplanning and prepping and turning them in early. Precrastinators are the typical "type A" personalities – list makers, organizers, and worst of all – ironers.

He conducts a series of experiments in the workplace, creating a scenario where different groups were given a problem to solve. One group was offered the chance to play the game Minesweeper during the time they had to ideate; the other group was not. It turns out that the group Adam calls the "moderate procrastinators" was 16% more creative than the group offered no distractions during the experiment. He was able to identify a pattern and a "sweet spot", in the amount of time a procrastinator was able to enhance their creativity, as opposed to hinder it by waiting until the last minute.

"It's only when you're told that you're going to be working on this problem, and then you start procrastinating but the task is still active in the back of your mind, that you start to incubate," Grant explains. "Procrastination gives you time to consider divergent ideas, to think in nonlinear ways, to make unexpected leaps."

But this actually makes perfect sense. We've learned that the human brain is an incredible machine that in many ways functions best when it's in "sleep" mode – this mode being either in an unconscious state like sleep or meditation, or when in a non-distracted environment like the shower, or in this case, playing a game that doesn't require active strategic thinking.

In other words, our CPU is our "HPU" – our Human Processing Unit – that enables anyone who is human to be creative. The trick, it seems, is to not let our active thinking get too much in the way and allow for the rumination of ideas to connect with others in a non-linear way.

My husband, Bryan, has found that his best ideas for funny social media posts come to him while he's out for a walk. Sometimes he wanders for hours, typing in whatever ideas come to him into Evernote on his phone. He keeps a running list of hilarious quotes from our kids and everyday interactions, as well as takes note of ridiculous and random things he observes while he's walking. He has learned that even if something doesn't make sense at the time, it may be a nugget of an idea that could become something later on, and everything is worth saving.

I write down my ideas in Simplenote on my phone, but also carry a small notebook in my purse. Sometimes, typing an idea doesn't fully allow me to get it all down since I am a visual thinker and use scribbled sketches to remind me of a thought. #Givememyquadpad

On Twitter, I use Social Jukebox to manage a set of scheduled Tweets (yes, a busy girl needs some automation, because... life). I subscribe to the "400+ Random Facts" list, which tweets out one random fact every few hours from my handle.

I am so entertained by these random facts, and am learning so much from my own damn Twitter feed! (I can't tell you how many times I'll go check my feed and love something so much I want to retweet it, then realize I tweeted it out in the first place OMG.) These facts also generate a lot of conversations with random people on Twitter, who respond to the facts with questions, funny comments or challenging the source. I'm always honest in my response, in including Social Jukebox's Twitter handle and asking them to verify the fact. So far – crickets – but I can only assume they have been vetted by someone. #goodenoughforme #winning

Bryan Kramer ✔ with Courtney Smith Kramer.
Yesterday at 10:39am · San Jose, CA ·

There's a lot of technology under our new bed. Takes a lot of hydraulics to handle what I've got.

Is that normal?

Everyone is weird. Aren't we all our own center of normal?! But when it comes to normal vs. weird, in reference to libido, it turns out there is no "normal" level of desire we humans are expected to benchmark against.

According to the website "The Greatist"[16], sex drive is a completely personal and individual experience. Depending on if it's at a jackrabbit or snail's pace, or somewhere inbetween, your libido is affected by a multitude of factors such as diet, hormone levels, past experiences, the health of your current relationship, and drugs and medication.

Libido only becomes an issue when the levels between you and your partner are not aligned – one is low and the other high – and it can lead to real tension in a relationship.

The good news is, changing your libido is solvable if you want/need it. At the end of the day, how much sex you're wanting to have should be up to you – not the media, and not anyone else.

And remember, it could be worse to be the exception instead of the rule. Did you know the longest female orgasm ever recorded was 120 excruciating minutes long?? Or, a British woman named Elle Anne has an orgasm about every 5 minutes, which averages about 250 a day! (And YOU thought grocery shopping was a nightmare.) After finally seeing her doctor, she was diagnosed with Permanent Sexual Arousal Disorder (PSAD?) and she was prescribed medication to help manage the disorder. Elle Anne's longest recorded orgasm was an earth-shattering and surely painful 83 minutes.[17] #AsLongAsTheKentuckyFriedMovie

16 http://greatist.com/grow/libido-concerns-treatment

BigHairedBarbie @BigHaired... 3h
But what if you had already
mourned 2 cats? What did you
shave off to mourn the next one?
#2manycats #catfacts
twitter.com/cshasarrived/s...

> **Courtney Smith** @cshasarrived
> Ancient Egyptians shaved off
> their eyebrows to mourn the
> deaths of their cats. #fact

Details

2. RANDOM
STRANGER
RESPONSE

1. TWEET JUKEBOX
RANDOM FACT

 Courtney Smith
@cshasarrived

.@BigHairedBarbie You served
up a pussy joke like a softball
girl...

6:04pm · 20 Jan 2016 · TweetDeck

||| VIEW TWEET ACTIVITY

3. OBVIOUS RETORT

All is not lost

More on this in *Reason #18: Do it every day*, but new studies show that having sex every day actually makes us more creative. #boom #waitforit #itscoming

How do you know if what you're having is quality sex? After all, why go the distance for something that's going to really suck? (unless there's actual sucking going on.) I learned in my research that there's a lot of click bait articles online that seem to want to answer this question, but most of them are from the perspective of new relationships, or young relationships. I can currently only speak for myself – in my mid-40s and having been married twice – so most of the advice I read about quality, I take with a grain of salt.

Ways you can presumably tell if you're getting a gold star in the bedroom included everything from dirty talk, to looking into each others' eyes, from lingering kisses, to not doing it "urgently and quietly". LOL. In the interest of not allowing the media to shape too much of anyone's self-esteem about their performance, I would say, does it make you happy? Are you communicating honestly and openly with your partner? I'm not a therapist and have a degree in advertising, but this just seems like common sense to me.

And just because… records

An 18th-century Russian woman holds the world record for having birthed the most children: 69, which she had over the course of 27 pregnancies that included sixteen pairs of twins, seven sets of triplets, and four sets of quadruplets. But she's outdone by the male record-holder for most kids, a Moroccan emperor who, according to the Guinness Book of World Records, sired "at least 342 daughters and 525 sons, and by 1721, he was reputed to have 700 male descendants."[18] #whohasthismuchtime

17 http://www.therichest.com/rich-list/the-biggest/5-longest-orgasms-ever-recorded/?view=all

THE CREATIVE PROCESS

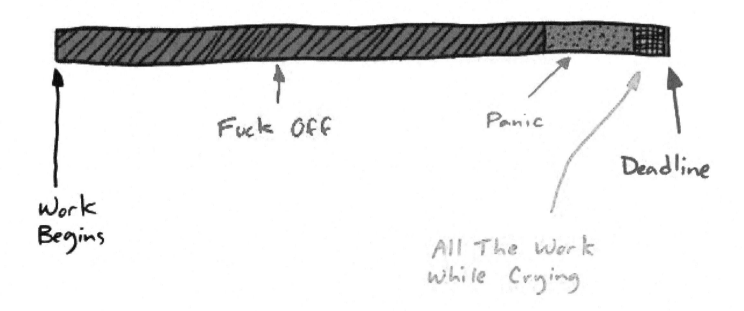

Work Begins

Fuck Off

Panic

Deadline

All The Work While Crying

Image drawn by Drew Fairweather of ToothpasteforDinner.com

mama NEEDS SOME wine

I MIGHT GO DOWN

The role of fear and rejection in creativity

Part of being a leader in business means presenting your ideas to groups of people. These people are not always coming from the same perspective as you, and may be what I call, a hostile crowd.

Presenting your precious ideas to people like this is akin to cutting your gut open with a butter knife, placing your innards onto the table, and asking with a smile on your face what everyone thinks of the quality of your health.

You think I'm kidding, but I'm not. Presenting my ideas that I've poured my heart and soul into is probably the most frightening thing I've ever had to do in my career. This fear has held me back from trying a lot of things I've wanted to do, and I've finally come to the point in my life where I'm not going to take it anymore! #QuietRiot

Here's the thing: Fear does not equal failure. Everyone has fear. The trick is turning your fear into courage, which is just being afraid and doing it anyway. The truth is, if you don't willingly choose to put yourself out there and fall down sometimes, others will try to push you down. I don't love this, because I have an inherent faith in humans to do the right thing. But the reality is, some people tear others down to make themselves feel better.

It's just a reality of life. #thingstosolveanotherday. So wouldn't you rather try to at least control the direction you fall, instead of letting others choose for you?

The more we allow ourselves to fail, misstep, and admit that things didn't quite go according to plan, the better our world will be. There are always an infinite set of possibilities for outcomes in addition to the one in our head. Perhaps serendipity has a different plan for us that's better – not necessarily easier – but no one ever learned by doing things the easy way.

"There is a deep and meaningful connection between risk taking and creativity and it's one that's often overlooked," contributor Steven Kotler wrote in Forbes. "Creativity is the act of making something from nothing. It requires making public those bets first placed by imagination. This is not a job for the timid. Time wasted, reputation tarnished, money not well spent -- these are all by-products of creativity gone awry."[19]

Squeeze the ball with your left hand

So what can you do to increase creativity when facing a fearful or stressful situation? According to a 2012 Study conducted by the American Psychological Association[20], "German researchers found that athletes can improve their performance under pressure simply by squeezing a ball or clenching their left hand before competition to activate the right side of the brain. Right-handed athletes who squeezed a ball in their left hand before competing were less likely to choke under pressure than those players who squeezed a ball in their right hand which activated the left hemisphere."

So, is the same true with sex? According to Binge[21], the testicles are covered by a muscle layer that extends up into the abdomen, so including them in the party can be extra

19 "18 Habits Of Highly Creative People" by Carolyn Gregoire
20 https://www.psychologytoday.com/blog/the-athletes-way/201304/squeeze-ball-your-left-hand-increase-creativity
21 http://www.bustle.com/articles/95475-what-to-do-with-his-balls-because-maybe-its-time-to-give-them-a-little-tug

THE "ICK" FACTOR

ACCIDENTALLY HITTING AN ADJACENT KEYBOARD CHARACTER CAN CHANGE THE MEANING OF WHAT YOU'RE TRYING TO SAY. IT'S ALSO THE QUICKEST WAY TO RECEIVE A CRYING EMOJI IN A TEXT MESSAGE.

YES, I HAVE DONE BOTH.

1) A PROJECT **KICK OFF** IS DIFFERENT THAN A PROJECT **LICK OFF**

2) GETTING **SICK** IS DIFFERENT THAN GETTING **DICK**

satisfying. But just how much, and exactly what, is still up for debate. Sam Phillips, a writer for LA Weekly conducted an informal open-ended survey on her Facebook page that returned as many different answers as the 5000+ friends in it, but concluded this. "Hold them but don't squeeze them, compliment them but ignore them, be gentle but scratch them, suck but don't suck them, fondle but don't rub them – and in some cases don't even touch them." It sounds to me that the very best thing is to just get creative, and see where your inspiration takes you. #ballsinyourcourt

Be invested in the action

Robert L Sternberg, co-author of "How to Develop Student Creativity", developed the investment theory of creative thinkers, as "Buying Low and Selling High". According to Sternberg, (and I can't do this justice describing this in my own words so much of this is quoted as an excerpt from his book):

> Creative people generate ideas that are like undervalued stocks (stocks with a low price-to-earning ratio), and both are generally rejected by the public. When creative ideas are proposed, they are often viewed as bizarre, useless, and even foolish, and are summarily rejected, and the person proposing them regarded with suspicion and perhaps even disdain and derision.

> Creative ideas are both novel and valuable. Why, then, are they rejected? Because the creative innovator stands up to vested interests and defies the crowd and its interests. The crowd does not maliciously or willfully reject creative notions; rather it does not realize, and often does not want to realize, that the proposed idea represents a valid and superior way of thinking. The crowd generally perceives opposition to the status quo as annoying, offensive, and reason enough to ignore innovative ideas.

Evidence abounds that creative ideas are rejected (Sternberg and Lubart 1995). Initial reviews of major works of literature and art are often negative. Toni Morrison's Tar Baby received negative reviews when it was first published, as did Sylvia Plath's The Bell Jar. The first exhibition in Munich of the Norwegian painter, Edvard Munch, opened and closed the same day because of the strong negative response from the critics.

Some of the greatest scientific papers are rejected by not one but several journals before being published. John Garcia, a distinguished biopsychologist, was IF AN IDEA IS WIDELY REJECTED BY MANY BUT CARRIED FORWARD BY ITS CREATOR WITH PASSION AND CONVICTION, THEY COULD BE ONTO SOMETHING. *summarily denounced when he first proposed that classical conditioning could be produced in a single trial of learning (Garcia and Koelling 1966).*

From the investment view, then, the creative person buys low by presenting a unique idea and attempts to convince other people of its value. After convincing others that the idea is worthy, which increases the perceived value of the investment, the creative person sells high by leaving the idea to others and moving to another idea. Although people typically want others to love their ideas, immediate universal applause for an idea usually indicates that it is not particularly creative.

I love this so very much, the notion that if an idea is widely rejected by many but carried forward by its creator with passion and conviction, they could be onto something. The excerpt concludes with this very important paragraph:

Foster creativity by buying low and selling high in the world of ideas—defy the crowd. Creativity is as much an attitude toward life as a matter of ability. We routinely witness creativity in young children, but it is hard to find in older children and adults because their creative potential has been suppressed by a society that encourages intellectual conformity. We begin to suppress children's natural creativity when we expect them to color within the lines in their coloring books.

Be a little out of line

Speaking of kids and creativity, Adam Grant in the New York Times[22] succinctly has this message to parents: Back the EFF off. (OK I added the expletive, but that's how strongly I feel about it.)

He theorizes that the reason why child prodigies rarely become adult geniuses who change the world, is because from a young age they've been taught and rewarded to incessantly practice and repeat the same structured tasks to conform to what others want and expect from them. "What holds them back is that they don't learn to be original. They strive to earn the approval of their parents and the admiration of their teachers. But as they perform in Carnegie Hall and become chess champions, something unexpected happens: Practice makes perfect, but it doesn't make new," he explains.

STOP ASKING YOUR KIDS WHAT THEY WANT TO BE WHEN THEY GROW UP. ASK THEM WHAT CHALLENGES THEY WANT TO SOLVE...

"Research suggests that the most creative children are the least likely to become the teacher's pet, and in response, many learn to keep their original ideas to themselves,"

Grant explains. In a society that celebrates "following the rules", this is counter-intuitive to the tomes preached by many schools in their desire to produce the best "innovators" and "brightest thinkers" in their communities. In Grant's very accurate words, "Creativity may be hard to nurture, but it's easy to thwart."

So what can we be doing as adults to nurture our children's creativity?

Grant offered a few pieces of key advice, based on his research:

1. The parents of ordinary children had an average of six rules, like specific schedules for homework and bedtime. Parents of highly creative children had an average of fewer than one rule. This causes children to think for themselves and focus on building their own moral code instead of following someone else's rules.

2. Don't dream of raising superstar kids. As important as it is to become an expert in a field, research indicates that the more we practice a skill, the more trapped we become in our thinking. It actually inhibits our ability to think creatively if the rules change.

3. Expose them to many environments that shape and inform their curiosities naturally – then support and encourage these intrinsic passions. Top performing scientists are also much more likely to dabble in performing arts, music and fine arts; not because they have to, but because they are naturally curious about them.

His best advice? "If you want your children to bring original ideas into the world, you need to let them pursue their passions, not yours."

And my advice? I don't know who said this but I saw it on Facebook and it stopped me in my tracks. "Stop asking your kids what they want to be when they grow up. Ask them what challenges they want to solve, then they can spend their time figuring out who to work with to get that done." #love

IT'S NOT THE LENGTH, IT'S THE GIRTH

Brevity is the soul of wit.

#enoughsaid

IT'S HOW IT MAKES YOU FEEL, NOT WHO'S DOING THE FEELING

A girl on girls

I've been in the creative arts field for over 25 years now, and have to say one thing – where are all the ladies?? The last time I checked, the overall world population skewed just slightly toward the female gender, and I am pretty sure all those women have brains, a sense of humor, problem-solving abilities, and – oh, BEE TEE DUBBYAH – the majority of purchasing decisions in American households. So why aren't there more women in creative positions?

According to new research published in September 2015 in Psychological Science[24], findings suggest that the work and achievements of men tend to be evaluated as more creative than similar work and achievements produced by women.

"Our research shows that beliefs about what it takes to 'think creatively' overlap substantially with the unique content of male stereotypes, creating systematic bias in the way that men and women's creativity is evaluated," says lead researcher Devon Proudfoot of the Fuqua School of Business at Duke University.

Yes, FUQUA that.

"This result suggests that gender bias in creativity judgments may affect tangible economic outcomes for men and women in the workplace," the researchers write. "In suggesting that women are less likely than men to have their creative thinking recognized, our research not only points to a unique reason why women may be passed over for corporate leadership positions, but also suggests why women remain largely absent from elite circles within creative industries," says Proudfoot.

You can see the infuriating trickle effect of simply judging ones creativity by gender. Less money. Less recognition. Less diversity. And much, much less opportunity to create new ways of thinking that could make the world a better, more balanced place.

I am sure none of this comes as no surprise to Kat Gordon[25], a former advertising agency copywriter who got sick and tired of seeing women creatives get left out of pitches and meetings. After owning her own agency that specialized in marketing to women, she founded the 3% Conference[26], with its mission laser-focused on increasing diversity in the workplace across industries.

On her website, she explains "The more varied the people who come up with ideas, the more varied the ideas will be. And since women control the majority of consumer spending and social sharing, it only makes sense to involve them in the creative process.

Yet, until we came along, **only 3% of Creative Directors were women.**" #boldforareason

WHAT THE… Yeouch. As a person of the female gender, who grew up wholeheartedly believing I was a creative person, and had just as much if not more to offer in this department that anyone else, this math does not add up.

She continues, "After years of wondering 'why isn't someone addressing this as the huge business issue it is?', Kat slowly realized that perhaps she was that someone. She began researching the many reasons why women only represent 3% of Creative Directors. Most of the issues start with a two-word phrase: lack of. Lack of support for motherhood, lack of mentorship, lack of awareness that femaleness is an asset to connecting to the consumer marketplace today, lack of celebration of female work due to gender bias of award juries, lack of women negotiating their first agency salary and every one thereafter."

Are you pissed yet?

I've had the pleasure of meeting Kat and talking with her about her work, and I absolutely love and support everything she's doing. But even now, 3 years after the 3% conference was launched and an official 3% Movement started, her annual conference is still only attracting audiences in the hundreds.

This is not an issue reserved for women in the creative fields; this is an issue about equality and opportunity to contribute and change the conversation. If the root reason is "lack of", let's all raise our voices and fill this void. Be the mentors, celebrate the work, put equality into practice and collectively feel the spoils of how this change feels, when ideas come together in unexpected ways that make us feel something.

Just like sex, it takes two genders to give something life.

At your prime: Considering age, creativity and sex

Remember when you were a kid and the thing that horrified you the most was walking in on your parents having sex? When you're in single digits, your parents are OLD and the thought of them getting jiggy is enough to make you puke. And you're convinced that the only reason why they'd be doing it anyway – something you can never unsee in your mind – was to make babies, and they surely didn't like it because they did it only the few times they had too. #shudderandgag

Thinking that age has anything to do with how much creativity, or sex, we experience is exactly as misinformed.

When it comes to creativity, we're all different in the times in our lives when it's maximized. Is it measured on productivity? Original outputs? Career-span? Dean Keith Simonton, Distinguished Professor of Psychology at the University of California Davis[27], says age and creativity can be assessed using these principles:

> *Some types of people, such as lyrical poets and mathematicians, tend to peak early and rapidly decline.*

> *Other types of people, such as historians and philosophers, are prone to later peaks with almost no decline.*

> *Some types are one hit wonders (fingers crossed to not be in this category)*

> *Some types are "highly prolific creators" who make continual creative contributions well into their 70s and beyond. #pickme*

27 Scientific American Mind, March/April 2016, pg. 70

BEDTIME CONVERSATIONS THAT CHANGE AS WE AGE.

20S. HONEY LETS TRY A STRAP ON.

30S. SHE NEEDS A NEW DIAPER ON.

40S. DUDE, PUT A NOSE STRIP ON.

Early bloomers tend to have their peak shifted forward.

Late bloomers who start later in life will see their pinnacle delayed – in fact, some do not truly hit their stride until their 60s or 70s. Actor Morgan Freeman earned his private pilot's license at age 65!

The big Cheery – O!

At least in England, more than half (54%) of men and almost a third (31%) of women over the age of 70 reported they were still sexually active, with a third of these men and women having frequent sex – meaning at least twice a month – according to data from the latest wave of the English Longitudinal Study of Ageing (ELSA)[28].

These numbers are consistent with a 2015 study of U.S. adults over 70, to the letter[29]. So, one could deduce that sex is an instinctual behavior for humans, and by the time we're in the autumn of life, at least roughly 40% of the age bracket is still wanting to rake that yard.

What I find interesting and consistent about both creativity and sex, is that both are inspired by what makes YOU passionate. True creativity is inspired by your unique energy that makes you excited; and great sex is experienced by your unique energy that makes you excited. The incredible thing about humans, is that the things that inspire creativity within you, and sexual feelings within you, are probably not the same things. Their paths don't ever have to cross, but the inspiration for both starts with what really makes us passionate.

Monkeying around: Species and sex

It turns out the second most sexual species on the planet behind humans is the Bonobos monkey[30] (formerly known as the Pygmy Chimpanzee), an endangered species that lives

28 http://www.manchester.ac.uk/discover/news/love-and-intimacy-in-later-life-study-reveals-active-sex-lives-of-over-70s/
29 Scientific American Mind, November/December 2015, pg. 17

in Central Africa. Unlike their close ape cousins, they abhor violence and instead use sexual behavior as the mechanism to enforce mores within their group, operating as a "Gynecocracy." This means "women's social supremacy", observed to exhibit Altruism, compassion, empathy, kindness, patience and sensitivity.

Bonobos are the only non-human animal to have been observed engaging in tongue kissing, and oral sex. Bonobos and humans are the only animals to typically engage in face-to-face genital sex. They are one of a handful of species on earth that partake in "penis fencing" – yes, it's a thing! – not as an act of aggression, but to cement bonds, reduce conflict, and express communal excitement over food. #Getthatawayfrommyfood

In essence, they are the hippies of the primate community, free love and all. Here are a few of the societal benefits we humans can learn from the Bonobos, as outlined by Dr. Christopher Ryan[31]:

YES, PENIS FENCING IS A REAL THING.

- **More sex equals less violence:** Bonobos use sex to avoid violence; The connection between less restrictive sexuality and less conflict generally holds true for human societies as well.

- **When females are in charge, there is a higher quality of life for everyone:** The combined sisterhood solidarity keeps the males in line, and lots of sex keeps them happy. "Each of the arguably smartest mammals – humans, chimps, bonobos, and dolphins – is promiscuous," says Dr. Ryan.

- **Good sex doesn't always include an orgasm, and casual sex doesn't mean "cheap":** Bonobos may be promiscuous, but it doesn't mean they're not romantic about it. They have been consistently observed kissing, holding hands and gazing

30 https://en.wikipedia.org/wiki/Bonobo
31 https://www.psychologytoday.com/blog/sex-dawn/201202/7-things-bonobos-can-teach-us-about-love-and-sex

into each other's eyes during sex, like humans. And most of their sexual greetings outside of intercourse are a quick "copping a feel".

- **Sex and food go great together:** I can't say it any better than Dr. Ryan: "Give a group of bonobos a bunch of food and they'll all have some quick sex before very politely sharing a meal."

Now that gives new meaning to "eating out"!

Your creativity will lead to wonderful achievements.

 YES NO

REASON #10 CREATIVITY IS LIKE SEX

SOMETIMES, IT'S FAKED

Debunking the myths vs. realities of creativity and sex

MYTH #1: ARTISTS ARE TORTURED AND CRAZY.

<preface> There is clearly an intertwining of "artists" with "creativity" in the studies I found, so for the purposes of clarity, I believe these statistics reference people in the creative arts – writers, artists, musicians, actors – but let's just assume everybody because I still believe that all it takes is a beating heart to qualify someone as "creative". <endpreface>

A recent study conducted in northern Europe by biological research company deCODE Genetics[32] studied the DNA of 80,000 "creative" people looking for genetic variants that increase the risk of bipolar disorder or schizophrenia. In a subset of 1000 "creative" people, they found a consistent variant of higher risk of 17-25% for mental illness. This wasn't the only study conducted to find a correlation between mental illness and artists; a 2012 study by the Journal of Psychiatric Research found that creative professionals are 8% more likely than the general population to be bipolar. "Writers are especially vulnerable, the researchers say, being 120 percent more prone to suffer from bipolar disorder. Writers were also more likely to abuse substances and take their own lives."

Feeling pretty great about being a writer right now. Did I mention I love wine?!

Shelley Carson, a Harvard professor and author of "Your Creative Brain", poses a different theory[33]: Creativity and mental illness share a process called "cognitive disinhibition." This means that both deliver the inability to filter out useless information, images and ideas from our environment out of our conscious awareness. For a mentally ill person, this can trigger confusion and an inability to cope. In a sane creative person, it could trigger new and interesting ideas, concepts and theories others can't see.

Cognitive disinhibition is part of a larger theory by Carson called "Shared Vulnerability" between creativity and psychopathy. She explains it this way. "When considering the "shared vulnerability" model, it's that two people can share behavioral and biological vulnerabilities without being alike. That's why not all creative people are a bit crazy and why not every mentally ill person is especially creative. It's not a one-on-one correspondence," says Carson. In fact, she says, most creative people don't exhibit severe mental problems at all; rather, the notable examples stick in our minds.

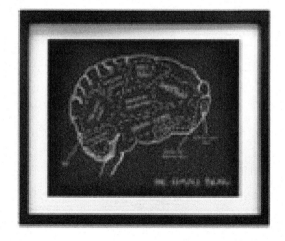

It's fun to archetype ultra-creative artists as mentally unstable. Like, Van Gogh cutting off his left ear as a romantic gesture. Or Lady Gaga wearing a meat dress to the VMAs, (which she did, as I found out for a very awesome reason, in protest to the military's 'Don't Ask, Don't Tell" policy against homosexuality. "If we don't stand up for what we believe in, if we don't fight for our rights, pretty soon we're going to have as much rights as the meat on our bones.") I think most geniuses border on crazy – but not because

33 http://www.fastcodesign.com/3021561/the-neuroscience-linking-creativity-and-mental-illness

they're mentally ill. Because they have the courage to be unconventional and stand up for what they wholeheartedly believe in, need to say, or to do. To people like that, NOT doing what they see in their heads is the torturous part.

So, are artists generally tortured and crazy? The jury is still out for me.

MYTH #2: CREATIVITY ONLY COMES FROM THE RIGHT SIDE OF YOUR BRAIN.

I was curious about the differences or similarities in how our brains think about things like art and science, when traditionally we've been told that we're either "right-brained"

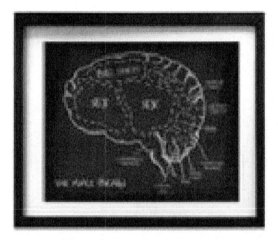

(creative) or left-brained (logical). How exactly does the brain organize itself when it comes to creativity in the arts and sciences?

The Imagination Institute, an independent non-profit organization based out of Philadelphia, is dedicated to making progress on the measurement, growth, and improvement of imagination across all sectors of society. According to their research, "We hypothesized that Openness should predict creative achievement in the arts, and intellect should predict creative achievement in the sciences. We focused on creative achievement—that is, formally recognized creative production—rather than on creativity more generally. Two factors relating to Openness (affective engagement and aesthetic engagement) were significantly associated with creative achievement in the arts, whereas two factors relating to Intellect (explicit cognitive ability and intellectual engagement) were significantly associated with creative achievement in the sciences."[34]

34 http://scottbarrykaufman.com/wp-content/uploads/2015/01/Kaufman-et-al.-2015.pdf "Openness to Experience and Intellect Differentially Predict Creative Achievement in the Arts and Sciences"

I think it's important to note that this study considered the *measurable* achievement of a creative act; In other words, the emergence of something tangible at the end of a creative act. In our day-to-day lives, however, we're not necessarily "achieving" acts of measurable creativity. Those particular manifestations take time and thought, resources and energy.

Math, science and art are so tightly tied to form, function and visualizations, that, in my opinion, the concepts of art and science are blurred. For instance, a carpenter designing a piece of furniture must consider its aesthetic, its form, materials, function, size and dimensions, in order to manifest it into existence. The sum of that experience is both art and science working in tandem to create something over time.

The September 2013 study, "Network Structure and Dynamics of the Mental Workspace"[35] published in the Proceedings of the National Academy of Sciences, conclude that human imagination does not come only from the right hemisphere of the cerebrum. In fact, creativity and imagination requires a widespread neural network in the brain. This mental workspace needed for creativity involves all four hemispheres of both the cerebrum and cerebellum[36].

So great news, self-selected left brained thinkers! You, too, can be creative. I don't buy that people are either right- or left-brained. I am convinced that our brains are so complex, receiving signals from visual, environmental, audible, historical and cognitive inputs that those synapses are rapid firing all over the damn place. I invite any of you experts to help me understand this more if you think I am wrong, as the more we know about our brains – the most powerful personal computer we will ever have – the more we can tap into its incredible power. #beammeup

35 http://www.pnas.org/content/110/40/16277.abstract
36 https://www.psychologytoday.com/blog/the-athletes-way/201508/why-does-overthinking-sabotage-the-creative-process

MYTH #3: DOING SOMETHING CREATIVE MAKE YOU HAPPIER

Good news… it's not a myth! The short answer is YES.

Experts say absolutely anyone can be creative, though different people may have different talents. "It really has to do with open-mindedness," says Dr. Carrie Barron, co-author of "The Creativity Cure," who says creativity applies to everything from making a meal to generating a business plan[37].

Creating something, varying your routine, doing something that makes you smile, it all leads to our human need to contribute, connect and be a part of something bigger than ourselves. How could that not make us happier?

MYTH #4: HAVING MORE SEX MAKES YOU HAPPIER

Carnegie Mellon recently conducted a study[38] trying to find this out. They asked 128 male/female partners to divide themselves into two groups: one, being asked to double the frequency of their weekly sex, and the other, with no directive other than to measure the frequency they naturally had sex. It turns out that after the study was complete, the group asked to double their weekly frequency reported being less happy than they were when they started. "It wasn't that actually having more sex led to decreased wanting and liking for sex. Instead, it seemed to be just the fact that they were asked to do it, rather than initiating on their own."

It turns out planning sex isn't fun (anyone trying to get pregnant can attest to this). But having it is fun. So the next time you want to be happy, go do it! Like, right now!

37 http://greatist.com/happiness/how-creativity-makes-us-happier
38 http://www.cmu.edu/news/stories/archives/2015/may/more-sex-does-not-lead-to-happiness.html

MYTH #5: UH-OH-OH-OH: WOMEN FAKE ORGASM. A LOT.

As reported in Psychology Today[39], "When in committed relationships, women and men experience orgasm with equal frequency. The answer is less biological than psychological–in committed relationships, men are more attentive, on average, to the sexual needs of their partners." Well, in a national sex study conducted by Indiana University[40], about 85% of men reported that their partner had an orgasm at the most recent sexual event; this compares to the 64% of women who reported having had an orgasm at their most recent sexual event.

Ummm… this math doesn't add up to me. Games should be upped here. Guys, a little more soft-handed windshield wiper action to the little friend between our legs goes a long way. Let's even up these numbers, shall we?

39 https://www.psychologytoday.com/blog/fulfillment-any-age/201207/6-myths-about-female-sexuality-and-why-theyre-wrong
40 National Survey of Sexual Health and Behavior (NSSHB) http://www.nationalsexstudy.indiana.edu/

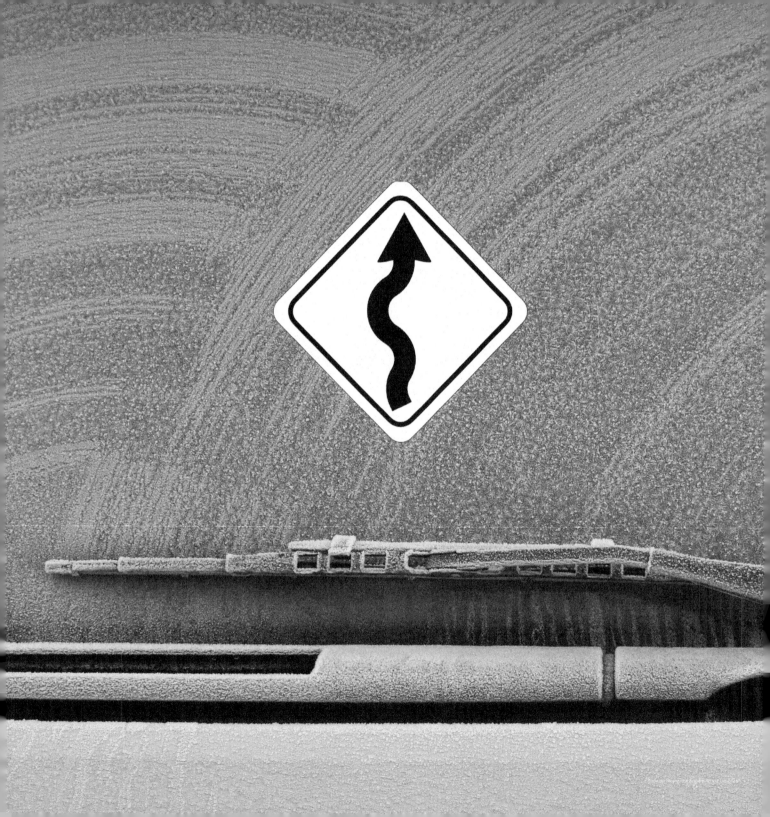

Touch

TOUCH THEM INSIDE

The importance of an emotional connection

According to Hockenberry and Hockenberry[41], an emotion is a "complex psychological state that involves three distinct components: a subjective experience, a physiological response, and a behavioral or expressive response." When you experience an emotion, you first frame what you're feeling into your own subjective context, with your experiences, beliefs, and values. Many experiences evoke mixed emotions that are seemingly polarized, like when you're waiting in line to ride a roller coaster, and you feel both scared and exhilarated at the same time. These feelings then evoke a physiological response; in the case of waiting in line for a roller coaster, this would be the waves of fluttering in your gut, sweaty palms, dry mouth and lightheadedness. These physical responses to this emotion are then expressed by maybe, shifting your weight from side to side, bending over to catch your breath, clapping your hands or squealing. (yes, as you might have deduced, this is exactly my manifestation of waiting in line for a roller coaster, something I don't do much anymore since I had kids and lost my reckless gene.)

There are a few models of emotions used to explain their innate complexity. The most widely used is Paul Eckman's "Six Basic Emotions"[42], developed from analyzing facial expressions from humans all over the world, across cultures. The universal emotions

41 Discovering Psychology, Textbook by Don H. Hockenbury and Sandra E. Hockenbury
42 https://en.wikipedia.org/wiki/Paul_Ekman

are: Anger, Disgust, Fear, Happiness, Sadness and Surprise. In 1990, he added some additional emotions, which are not detectable through facial expressions: Amusement, Contempt, Contentment, Embarrassment, Excitement, Guilt, Pride in Achievement, Relief, Satisfaction, Sensory pleasure, and Shame.

"When we see someone experiencing an emotion (be it anger, sadness, happiness, etc), our brain "tries out" that same emotion to imagine what the other person is going through," says Steve Parton from CuriousApes.com. "And it does this by attempting to fire the same synapses in your own brain so that you can attempt to relate to the emotion you're observing. This is basically empathy. It is how we get the mob mentality, where a calm person can suddenly find themselves picking up a pitchfork against a common enemy once they're influenced by dozens of angry minds. It is our shared bliss at music festivals, or our solidarity in sadness during tragedies."[43]

It's also probably why I cried every time I watched someone "have a moment" on American Idol (not because I am secretly blinded by Ryan Seacrest's awesomeness #sorrynotsorry).

In fact, music, as an expression of creativity, has a profound effect on us humans – including, as it turns out so very conveniently for my book – making us have more sex. Fast Company reports that "insofar as technology has made music easier to create, find, and listen to, the very same networks and gadgets that seem to drive us apart may actually wind up making us feel closer, both physically and emotionally. And yes, that includes sex."[44]

A recent study conducted jointly by Apple Music, Sonos and Daniel Levitan, author of *This is Your Brain on Music* followed 30 households who spent one week listening to music using personal headphones, followed by a week of playing music openly and freely throughout the house using speakers.

43 http://psychpedia.blogspot.com/2015/11/the-science-of-happiness-why.html?m=1
44 http://www.fastcompany.com/3056554/how-music-changes-our-behavior-at-home?utm_source=mailchimp&utm_medium=email&utm_campaign=tech-weekly-newsletter-featured&position=1&partner=newsletter&campaign_date=02172016

The difference in their interactions with each other as familial units was astonishing.

"When music is playing openly at home, people become physically closer," Levitan said. "The average distance between household members decreased by 12% during the in-home study. In the U.S., housemates (usually family members), spent four and a half more hours together with music playing than without it. With music on, people were 33% more likely to cook together and 85% more likely to invite people over. They were 15% more likely to laugh together and 18% more likely to utter the words 'I love you.'" And naturally as mentioned earlier, they also have more sex. The initial survey reported that couples were 66% more intimate when music is playing, spending 37% more "awake time" in bed. **Make a note to yourself now: BUY SPEAKERS IMMEDIATELY #YoureWelcome**

I love your shape

I am fascinated with the science of sound – or Cymatics – something I was introduced to years ago when we were working with Plantronics. It turns out that sound vibration at different frequencies causes particles in water and other matter, like sand or oil, to organize themselves into different fractal shapes. When you change the frequency of a sound, the patterns literally change in front of you, organizing themselves into completely different beautiful sacred geometric shapes. Google "CYMATICS: Science Vs. Music - Nigel Stanford" on YouTube and be prepared to have your brain broken. Like, I'm talking secret to the Universe shit here.

If you're a spiritual person, also Google the video that shows the cymatic shapes of the Buddhist word "Om". According to Samantha Allen, an editorial writer for DoYouYoga[45], "Om" is said to be the manifestation and name of the God who created the universe. Before "Om", there was only an empty void. The vibration of "Om" filled that space, much the same way that the elliptical orbits of planets fill our solar system." I'll give you one guess as to the shape the "Om" sound makes when played near organic material. Yup… two concentric ellipses – the exact same shape as our own solar system. #universemicdrop

Since I can't show you the video, here are some of the absolutely stunning, spirographic-like shapes sound vibration creates in organic matter[46].

And organic matter includes the human body. The brain and heart are composed of 73% water, and the lungs are about 83% water. The skin contains 64% water, muscles and kidneys are 79%, and even the bones are watery: 31%.[47] You saw the effect sound vibration had on water if you watched that Cymatics video, so no wonder, when we hear a piece of music that's vibration evokes a sentimental or sad emotion, it is LITERALLY tugging at your heart! It also explains why, when we hear certain beats, we can't help but get up and dance. Or at least tap our feet or hands to the music. The vibration is affecting the composition of the shapes of the cells in our bodies, provoking us to get up and move. Isn't this fascinating???!

Great creative always moves you

It's important to understand human emotions, as it's how we can connect with each other deeply through expression, without need for verbal communication. It's a basic human need to connect, develop relationships, feel loved and acknowledged, and advance ourselves, spiritually and intellectually.

It's also a key component to connective storytelling, and the great writers and orators know that if you want your story to be remembered, people have to feel touched on the inside to feel a connection at all.

46 Image courtesy of Tumblr TumbNation
47 http://water.usgs.gov/edu/propertyyou.html

Meg LeFauve, who wrote on both *Inside Out* and *The Good Dinosaur* for Pixar, says that one of her practices is to connect with characters through their vulnerability[48]. "Riley [from Inside Out] and Arlo [from The Good Dinosaur] are both around the same age and they're both coping with a loss that feels bigger than what they can handle. So it's really looking at how I felt when I was 11, or anybody in the room, and what that felt like then, or what loss feels like to us now. That kind of vulnerability always says a lot about a character and who they are specifically. At the same time, it's also about calibrating emotions so that they're not just that singular emotion all the time."

I think understanding how to connect through emotion is also why J.K. Rowling, writer of the "Harry Potter" series, is so skilled at her storytelling. In her books, she vividly describes the movie she sees in her head. If you think about the level of description she goes into when she's talking about the vulnerabilities of the characters, how they're feeling and their surroundings, I'm willing to bet that if you saw the movies after you read the books, you thought, "Oh, my God. It's exactly how I pictured it in my head."

Understanding emotional intelligence

Being aware of our emotions not only helps our own creative interpretation of experiences, but also helps us better express empathy toward others. Empathy is one of five components of "Emotional Intelligence" (EI), or the indicators increasingly used as the "X-factor" of strong leaders[49]. The five components are:

- Self-awareness: Knowing ones strengths, weaknesses, drives, values and impact on others

- Self-regulation: Controlling or redirecting disruptive impulses and moods

48 http://m.fastcompany.com/3053961/7-tips-on-emotional-storytelling-pixar-style-from-the-writer-of-inside-out-and-the-good-dino?utm_source=mailchimp&utm_medium=email&utm_campaign=cocreate-weekly&position=2&partner=newsletter&campaign_date=12032015

- Motivation: Relishing achievement for its own sake

- Empathy: Understanding other people's emotional makeup

- Social skill: Building rapport with others to move them in the desired direction

Much like creativity, many have argued that either a person is born with EI or not. But more research is surfacing that everyone has varied capability to be Emotionally Intelligent, and the skills can be honed with practice.

EI and sex

Much like sex, the components of EI also translate to what people have cited as the criteria for choosing who they want in the sack. When it comes to picking a mate, humans are by far the most creative.

In every culture around the world, over 90% of people choose to marry at least once[50]. And the criteria of choosing these mates is expected, but also biased; an obvious one, proximity, topped the list. Men seem

ACROSS CULTURES, THE TOP TWO CHARACTERISTICS PEOPLE DESIRE IN AN 'IDEAL MATE' ARE KINDNESS AND INTELLIGENCE.

to prioritize youthful and attractive appearance, and health, over financial success and education; women, the opposite. According to Hockenbury and Hockenbury, "In fairness, evolutionary psychologists do not consider humans to be mindless robots controlled by rigid genetic forces. Humans are the most flexible of creatures, so even if millions of years of sexual selection have shaped our mating preferences and strategies for choosing a mate, we should still expect a wide range of human behavior that adapts itself to new situations.

49 Daniel Goreman, Harvard Business Review, Summer 2014
50 http://bcs.worthpublishers.com/discoveringpsych6e/#831452__855677__

Also, we should not be discouraged by research that emphasizes the role of physical attractiveness, youth, financial resources, or status in attracting a mate. In David Buss's international survey, none of these characteristics was consistently ranked at the top of the desirability list. Across cultures, the top two characteristics people desire in an 'ideal mate' were kindness and intelligence. And finally, remember that no matter what characteristics people desire in an 'ideal mate,' they generally marry someone who is similar to them on all dimensions." #Dadbodiesrejoice

From need to drive

The six basic human psychological needs – love/connection, certainty, uncertainty, significance, growth and contribution – are the motivators behind our emotions, reactions and behavior since the dawn of time. But cultural shifts in attitudes toward sex, and everything that surrounds it (who we can have it with, how we do it, what circumstances should be in place to have it), has created a massive evolution in how sex is even classified in our human psyche.

All of the emotionally charged belief systems are at play here. Homosexuality. Sadism. Marriage. Promiscuity. Masturbation. Polygamy. Cultural attitudes and who we choose for our own human tribes determine the guardrails around these activities. But also the subtle – if any – differences between men and women's emotional needs for a relationship and picking a mate as well. There have even been countless studies that seem to suggest that women are "evolutionarily helpless" in their need to have an emotional connection to their partner in order to have sex; even, as suggested in some cases, to become aroused at all, because "men have a virtually unlimited supply of sperm to propagate, but women have precious few eggs to be fertilized."[51]

First of all, any study that suggests women are evolutionarily incapable of doing anything compared to men can suck it. And yeeeahhhh, I know for me, fertilizing eggs are the first and most sexy thing I could ever think of before sex. #saidnooneever

Mark Manson, author of *Models: Attract Women Through Honesty*[52] and *The Subtle Art of Not Giving a Fuck* explains why people aren't getting it right when they refer to sex as a "need".

> *"Men and women get caught up in their own needs and then project those needs onto everyone around them. Women see men as cold and brutish because they expect them to have the same need for connection that they have. Men see women as manipulative and deceitful because they assume women use sex as a tool for self-esteem like they do. In both cases, they're wrong and mischaracterizing the people lying naked in front of them."*

Hmmmmm. He does say "lying in front of them", so maybe we can assume he's approaching the gender perspective from a more traditional view? But knowing that as humans, we embody each of the six basic human needs (with connection being, for the most part, the strongest when it comes to relationships) and that emotions are comprised of a subjective, physiological and expressive response, we can deduce that Mr. Manson may be onto something that could really help a lot of people better frame how they feel about sex.

He concludes:

> *"While sex is absolutely a physiological function, and in some ways it's no different than eating or crapping, evolution has intertwined our drive for sex (note: a drive,*

51 https://www.sharecare.com/health/sex-and-relationships/emotion-related-womans-sexual-arousal
52 http://markmanson.net/sex-and-our-psychological-needs

not a need) with our psychological needs for esteem and connection. Sex is not like eating, because a) you don't die without it, and b) it's inevitably an emotional experience when you have it. Nature has cleverly wired us this way — to put our psychological needs first and then use sex to fulfill them in order to trick us into sticking around and taking care of one another. Sure, we may still try to get a little sumthin' sumthin' on the side now and again. And sure, when we break up and feel crappy, we may go on a little sex spree to feel good about ourselves. But that's just it. It's not about the sex, it's about how we feel about ourselves. That's the way nature made it. And it's not changing any time soon."

Keep in mind, we're just talking about sex here, not love.

But does what he's describing define romantic love as "sex with a connection that incentivizes us to stick around and take care of each other"? Is it possible that what we call "love", is really just describing how *you* feel when you're with someone? And even deeper, does it explain why people can fall out of love just as easily as in it, because either you changed and felt different around someone, or they changed, and as a result, you feel different? #IfLoveFellinaForestWouldAnyoneHearIt #ItsNotYouItsMeIsReal

Now I need to know. What the heck is love?!

DO IT WITH MORE PARTNERS

May the force be with you

When you Google "What do people want out of a romantic partnership?", it returns over 28 million results. And when you scroll and start assessing the links, there are a lot of things written about relationships themselves – how do you know it's healthy, what even is a healthy relationship, what do humans need out of a relationship. There's lots of science, and studies, and quotes from experts.

But the one thing I didn't find, was a definitive definition of love.

Psychology Today[53] defines love as "a force of nature". Wow. That's pretty profound. Like the wind, love can only be observed, in its affect on others as it's happening. The article explains that "Sexual stimulation and gratification, whether by way of fingers, mouths, objects, fantasy play, whips and chains, or just plain intercourse, can certainly be bought and sold, not to mention used to sell other things. Whether sex should be for sale is another question entirely, but love itself cannot be sold.

One can buy loyalty, companionship, attention, perhaps even compassion, but love itself cannot be bought. An orgasm can be bought, but love cannot. It comes, or not, by grace, of its own will and in its own timing, subject to no human's planning." #literally #LoveisLiketheWindPatrickSwayzeNailedIt

53 https://www.psychologytoday.com/blog/love-without-limits/201111/what-is-love-and-what-isnt

When it comes to creativity, the same parallels can be drawn. Creativity is a force of nature, only observed in its affect on others as it's happening. Creative stimulation and gratification (or, expressions of ones creativity), whether by way of music, stories, art, architecture, or just plain positive problem solving, can certainly be bought or sold, not to mention used to sell other things. Whether these creative things should be for sale is another question entirely, but creativity itself cannot be sold.

> CREATIVITY IS A FORCE OF NATURE, ONLY OBSERVED IN ITS AFFECT ON OTHERS AS IT'S HAPPENING.

It comes, or not, by grace, of its own will and in its own timing, subject to no human's planning.

Well, shit. That kinda sucks. How the heck are we going to get done what we need to get done?! Is it really impossible to conjure up the exact type and expression of creativity you need in exactly the moment you need it?

Time to call our muses.

A-muse me. Like, now.

The original nine muses in Greek mythology were the goddess daughters of Zeus and Mnemosyne, all of whom presided over the arts and sciences. In modern day terms, a muse is a person who inspires creativity in others – and is almost always a woman. "From a creativity perspective, it is the feminine nurturing energy which enthuses our entire being, including our organs of sexuality, and gives rise to our creative passion to create."[54] The common tie between feminine energy and passion is the bridged connection between identifying with what you love in your heart, to the manifestation of this passion into the physical world. This is "muse as a metaphor" for inspiring ourselves to conjure what we truly love within our own hearts and grounding our ability to make it so here on earth. When you think of creativity in these terms – making something out of nothing – it really does sound magical, mythical, and powerful.

And it is. It is said when you stir the creativity inside your heart, it unleashes the most powerful energy in the universe, which includes sexual energy, to yourself and those around you.

Is it me, or is it getting hot in here?

I love the word "muse" so very much. As a noun, it represents inspiration, but as a verb, it means to think about an idea; not just for a second or a minute, but to ruminate over it for a very, very long time. It's not just a fleeting thought, but an ongoing pondering of an idea or concept that will not leave you alone until it finds its way into the world.

"21 Reasons Creativity is Like Sex" is my muse, that I have mused about for years. If I wasn't creating something that related to it, it would slow knock at the closed doors in my brain until I had no choice but to answer its calling. SO.ANNOYING. But awesome at the same time. Staying with this idea and finding new ways to express it has been joyful and painful and fulfilling and frustrating. Sounds a lot like love to me.

What, or who, is your muse? Don't sweat it if you don't know the answer right now. The good thing is that there are other humans around us on this planet, and chances are that if you're not experiencing creativity of its own will and in its own timing, someone else is, and that can be inspirational too.

This is why we need more partners. Partners who we trust, who willingly share their own moments of inspiration in order to inspire us, all in an effort to get a little closer to creativity gracing itself more often than not on us humans. #exhale

How do you know you're ready for a creative partner?

We've all been in a situation where we needed a little help. After Bryan and I had been married for about a year, we had to have an appliance fixed that had broken. I asked him if he knew how to fix it, and he said "hold on, let me get out my tool belt." He reached into his back pocket and pulled out his wallet. "Here it is. Now, who do we call to get it done?"

The same is true when it comes to exercising your creativity. Sometimes you just need to partner with someone to help creatively solve a problem.

No longer is it an economy of having to do things yourselves that you can't stand to do or aren't skilled enough to know how to do it right. The rise of the DIY (Do it Yourself) movement I believe exploded into mainstream because, thanks to technology, we no longer have to fill our time performing tasks we don't want to do. The ingenuity of connecting technologies with communities has made it possible for businesses like Task Rabbit and Thumbtack to enable us to pay someone to go stand in line for us at the movies, so we can do something else with our time. #BRILLIANT

And because in most modern day societies, we don't have to fill our time trying to merely survive, (unless you're on that show 'Naked and Afraid', where you and a stranger are plunked into the middle of nowhere buck naked with just a map and one survival item, of which most people choose to bring something useful, like a pot or firestarter, but truthfully, if I were in the wilderness for 21 days, my inclination would be to bring a pair of tweezers, because, you know, hair) we have a lot more time to ponder stuff.

Cool stuff, like the origin of DNA and why are we here, and are we alone in the Universe? Will that watermelon explode if I put it in the freezer? Why is there always only one shoe on the side of the road? Why does a plastic bat always find it's way to a man's crotch when a little kid swings it? And why is it always caught on video?! I digress.

I need a pro

A good way to know when you need a little professional creative problem solving help is like asking how do you know when it's time to stop making your own clothes and start buying them at the store? Some people are really great at sewing their own clothes. They may be expert designers who have created a demand for what they're selling. They've built a runway in their living room! They don't need no stinkin store.

But some people suck at sewing. They've been poked to death by needles. They run with scissors. They tried to make their own clothes but learned the hard way that they're just store people. They're willing to spend the money on the clothes because they're sick of standing naked in their living room. That's when you know you're ready to hire a professional creative partner. When you're standing naked and bleeding in your living room.

Lucky numbers

When it comes to sex, it seems the lucky number of partners most people have in their lifetime is lower than you'd think. According to a survey of adults aged 20 to 59, women have an average of just four sex partners during their lifetime, and men, an average of seven.[55]

What?? I'm calling bullshit. Clearly the people who participated in this study never went to college, lived in Roman times, or grew up in the 70s/80s/90s/2000s.

A QUICKIE IS NICE, BUT NOT EVERY TIME

Wait for it

I am a huge fan of serendipity. It makes me feel something magical is just around the corner that will surprise and delight me. And as much as I like structure and am a planner, making room for serendipity in your life makes you feel like a kid again.

I think the same is true for creativity. Allowing the room for an idea to silently incubate can return some seriously magical results. But in a world chock full of deadlines, this can seem hard to do – which often leads to the temptation to take whatever idea comes first, and run with it. Take it from me, from my own experience and as much as it pains me to speak the truth, most of the time, your first idea is the *worst*. We want it to be great. In the moment, it seems brilliant! But after more digging, research and a little more time to incubate, you realize just how ridiculous, mundane and trite it probably was.

I remember back in my first job as a young designer, I was tasked with coming up with a concept for a healthcare company print ad. In the creative brief, it said the objective was something like "To provide its patients with peace of mind that everything would be taken care of." #saideveryhealthcarecompanyever

I was so excited to work on a REAL project for REAL money, and was ready to put my shiny new degree to work. I sat with my sketch pad and pencil and started to brainstorm some creative ideas that might tell this important story in the right way. I explored my mind, trying to figure out what I could possibly come up with that people would visually understand. I needed a metaphor. A commonly understood story. It needed to be amazing! Wait! I had it! Puzzle pieces! I could show a photo of a patient and then make it look like a puzzle had been put together! YES! That was it! I did it!

Um… no. The unfortunate thing was, the idea made it through to show the client. And man, was I horrified to learn after that presentation that not only had they already tried this concept, but just about every one of their competitors had too. DOH! My confidence was crushed – but the best lesson learned. Not only had I not done my research, I had also stopped at the first idea. Did the solution work? Sure. Would it have stood out in a magazine against their competition? No way in hell. It was a problem solved, but not in a positive way in this context. It was not a *creative* solution, it was a first idea solution.

So why is this? We are educated, experienced, and smart people. Why shouldn't we be able to automatically spit out great ideas like little brainiac factories?? It's because coming up with great ideas takes practice, perspective, and persistence.

The power of practice, perspective and persistence

James Clear, a writer, entrepreneur and Behavioral Scientist, told a great story in his 2014 article in Entrepreneur Magazine[56] about author Markus Zusak. Markus had an idea for a book, and did the necessary preparation to set the construct and narrative how he wanted.

"When Zusak began to write out the story itself, he tried narrating it from the perspective of Death. It didn't come out the way he wanted. He re-wrote the book, this time through the main character's eyes. Again, something was off. He tried writing it from an outsider's perspective. Still no good. He tried present tense. He tried past tense. Nothing. The text didn't flow," Clear explains.

"He revised. He changed. He edited. By his own estimation, Zusak rewrote the first part of the book 150 to 200 times. In the end, he went back to his original choice and wrote it from the perspective of Death. This time—the 200th time—it felt right. When all was said and done it had taken Zusak three years to write his novel. He called it 'The Book Thief'."

Rewrote the book 150 to 200 times. This is not something we think about while reading the final work – but I am sure had he not, we might have been thinking that the book was a good read, but nothing special. It's like stepping onto an ice rink once a year and trying to do a Triple Lindy (not to be confused with the #5 Most Dangerous Sex Position, please especially don't try that on ice #moredangerous). You can't expect to be a pro if you only do it once a year #TWSS

NO SINGLE ACT WILL UNCOVER MORE CREATIVE POWERS THAN FORCING YOURSELF TO CREATE CONSISTENTLY. ~ JAMES CLEAR

The pros are the ones who make it look easy.

Clear continues. "In an interview after his book was finally released, Zusak said, 'In three years, I must have failed over a thousand times, but each failure brought me closer to what I needed to write, and for that, I'm grateful.' Grateful, I would say, is not at all, all. Clear reports that the book stayed on the New York Times best-seller list for over 230 weeks. It sold 8 million copies. It was translated into 40 languages. A few years later, Hollywood came calling and turned *The Book Thief* into a major motion picture.

Keep trying and eventually you'll find the sweet spot. #TWSS

So, practice, perspective, and persistence. Zusak embodied all three:

Practice: Rewriting a narrative up to 200 times is definitely great practice.

Perspective: Writing the narrative from multiple viewpoints helped him intimately understand how each character – including Death – approached the story. Understanding their motivations, values, outcomes and emotions about the story helped shape a more authentic dialogue and characterization, which allows us to lose ourselves in the story as opposed to simply observe it happening before us.

Persistence: He never gave up until his story sounded like what he needed to say.

As a human, you can understand practice and persistence. But how can you gain perspective to enhance your creativity, especially if you're not an author who can write a story from multiple viewpoints?

Travel, for one. Traveling outside your environment, your friend circle, other "like" points of view, is one of the best ways to gain a broader understanding of where others not like you are coming from.

I am writing this chapter (my final chapter, in fact, although not chronologically in this book) at 30,000 ft. returning from a 3-week European trip of a lifetime that my parents took me and my family on to celebrate their 50th wedding anniversary. We started in Amsterdam, where we boarded a Viking River Cruise and sailed down multiple rivers through Germany, Austria, Slovakia and ended in Budapest, then drove to Prague to round out our trip. We saw windmills, castles, cathedrals, fortresses, memorials, cafes, hamlets, huge cities, even medieval chastity belts.

RUSSIAN LOUNGE SINGER PHOTOBOMB

MY MOM

MY DAD

← SHE MAKES JEWELRY
SHE MADE THIS

The heavy part of the book

I am returning with a new understanding about World War II, having learned about it from both German and Allied Forces' historical exhibits close to Germany, from tour guides as well as next generation locals who remember their parents talking about the war from their perspective. Now I understand that it was very, very complicated. In school, we learn a very linear timeline about these things, taking it for fact and hearing it but not listening or understanding the true human emotion and motivations behind decisions.

I learned that the war started in the mid-1930s for most of Europe, with Hitler in the early days building his power in Germany. I always questioned what kind of people could have followed such a monster, but learned that in the early days, most of the people in Germany were poor, hungry, and desperate for a leader. They needed to believe the words of a young Hitler, who promised to make Germany the greatest country in the world. They did not know what they were signing up for.

I was reminded that in the hands of a few despicable people, hundreds of thousands of people died, persecuted for living a life they believed in. I learned that this has happened before many times – to the Celts, by the Romans, to the Turks, to the Hapsbergs, Napoleon, to Hitler, even to more modern day Czech Republic and Slovakia, a country that separated in the early 1990s when Communism fell.

Time and again on our trip, I was reminded about the dichotomy we have lived for centuries, in taking away life so very often without a mindful thought about the value of it. Death – eluding it, fearing it, mourning it – is a cycle that has not changed since the dawn of time.

For me, layers of humanity, history, love, tragedy, family, relationships, moments, laughter, sadness, despair and elation all came together in these three weeks. I am also married to a Jewish man, so the historical recount and walking the path, so-to-speak, of the people who were killed in the "during math" was magnified for me.

To be at Terrazin, a work camp in the Czech Republic, and walk where over 60,000 Jews, homosexuals, Christians and any other people who were interred for not believing what the Nazis did, was, in a very weak word, indescribable. The incinerators worked 24/7, for years, to dispose of the daily dead. Yet the prisoners made the most of it, from the recounts, and managed to create some incredible works of art, music, and theatre, to make life bearable.

The human spirit celebrates life, even in the face of death, which is constant.

You can see this experience had a heavy weighted effect on me. It altered my perspective, not only about the people of the past, but also made me more aware and observant of the life around me.

I saw that children are the same, no matter the language, or belief or nationality. They all play, laugh, are shy, and have meltdowns in the worst places. Come to think of it, parents dealing with a child's public meltdown act the same too – helpless, embarrassed, and trying to be as patient and cool-headed as they can, as to not disturb those around them.

We are a global society of connected humans. From Budapest, to the serene, quiet narrow rivers in the Netherlands, people on the shore or standing on the beautiful twinkling bridges overhead would wave excitedly with huge smiles on their face as we passed by.

"Hello!!" they would shout in English, or "Hoi!" in Dutch. It reminded me that we're all bound together by our curiosity, wanderlust and desire to connect to our space, our environment, and to each other.

Our first human instinct is to connect in a friendly way. How does it go so friggen awry sometimes?!

Enjoy the ride as you go.

OK, everyone, deep breath. Stand up, sit down, turn around, wipe off the slime and regroup. This is supposed to be a chapter about giving things time, so I'll get back to the lighter stuff.

If you need a quickie, here's some help

In case your passport is expired, or you are a homebody, there are some shortcuts you can take to get to a great idea more quickly.

The kind folks at DIYToolkit.com created an "Idea Generator" worksheet[57] that you can use to think about things differently, in an effort to improve your creative outcomes. When I saw this, I loved that it's a solid construct for asking the right questions about a problem/challenge, in order to get to the creative and not obvious solutions more quickly.

Try this out the next time you need to come up with some really choice solutions. You'll get there faster using this tool, I guarantee it. #TWSS

What if it's super short?

Not everyone is Sting, the British born singer from the Police who claims to use the powers of the Kama Sutra to have sex sessions lasting up to 8 hours long. Um… what??!! Who has time for that?? I love me a good romp, but there are Game of Thrones and Long Island Medium episodes to watch, people. I think there's a sponsorship opportunity for Camelback hydration pouches for you, Sting. #Justsayin

57 http://diytoolkit.org/tools/fast-idea-generator-2/

I want to generate new ideas
by thinking differently

FAST IDEA GENERATOR

THE APPROACH			THE NORMAL RULE	BENDING, BREAKING & STRETCHING THE RULE
∧	Inversion	Turn common practice upside down	Doctors treat patients	What if patients became doctors?
∫	Integration	Integrate offer with other offers	People access a range of services in different locations	What if different local services had one point of access?
✕	Extension	Extend the offer	Schools provide learning opportunities to children and young people during the day	What if schools also offered sport and recreation and community learning provision out of hours?
∂	Differentiation	Segment the offer	There is a 'one size fits all' approach	What if a service was personalised and differently segmented?
＋	Addition	Add a new element	Supermarkets deliver groceries	What if supermarkets delivered groceries and also provided hot meals to older people in their homes?
－	Subtraction	Take something away	Prisons are critical to an effective criminal justice system	What if you had to close three prisons?
t	Translation	Translate a practice associated with another field	Hospitals and airports are different kinds of operations	What if airport management practices were applied to hospitals?
g	Grafting	Graft on an element of practice from another field	Teaching and coaching are separate practices	What if coaching were introduced as part of secondary school education?
∞	Exaggeration	Push something to its most extreme expression	Schools support children and young people to learn, but only within designated times and in a designated space	What if students could access learning anytime and anywhere they chose?

The truth is, there is varying research about what is "average" for the time it takes to start and finish a good go in the sack. According to Medical Daily, "The findings revealed the average time for each couple, across all the times they had sex, ranged from 33 seconds to 44 minutes. Meanwhile, the average across all couples was 5.4 minutes. This means a couple will typically go for an average of 5.4 minutes every time they have sex."[58]

> Side note: "An average of 33 seconds to 44 minutes"?? I call that a "Krange", which is a combination of "Kramer" and "range" and stems from the ridiculously large ranges Bryan throws out when people ask him how much something will cost to do. His answer is usually "anywhere from one to a million dollars," because, #scoping. And, another side note: If average is 5.4 minutes, why is the average porn scene more than 20 minutes? #makesnosense #askingforafriend

WebMD has a more common-sensical explanation. "… A quick trigger is normal," says Ian Kerner, Ph. D. "Men are wired to ejaculate quickly – and stressful situations make them ejaculate even more quickly. It's been important to the human race. If guys took an hour to ejaculate, we'd be a much smaller planet."

Here's to the sustainability of the human race.

58 http://www.medicaldaily.com/how-long-does-sex-last-average-time-penis-shape-381025

LET'S GET ALL ~IPITY UP IN HERE

SERENDIPITY: AN UNEXPECTED PLEASANT SURPRISE.

SERENDIPITY AND SEX: THE SUDDEN EMERGENCE OF A FRESHLY MADE CLUB SANDWICH THE MINUTE YOU'RE FINISHED.

ZEMBLANITY: THE OPPOSITE OF SERENDIPITY; AN UNEXPECTED, UNPLEASANT SURPRISE.

ZEMBLANITY AND SEX: FUZZILY WAKING UP NEXT TO A STRANGER YOU THOUGHT WAS A DEAD RINGER FOR BRADLEY COOPER THE NIGHT BEFORE, BUT WAS MORE LIKE ALICE COOPER IN THE LIGHT OF DAY.

BAHRAMDIPITY: THE SUPPRESSION OF SERENDIPITOUS SURPRISES.

BAHRAMDIPITY AND SEX: MORMONS.

FANTASIZING MAKES IT GLORIOUS

Be tri-curious: Fantasy, daydreams and imagination

I have always believed that our minds are our sexiest assets. From the physical changes that happen in our bodies when we experience arousal, to the mental images we conjure to elicit these changes, our imaginations are a limitless source of fantasy, daydreams, and curiosity-led adventure to explore.

According to English philosopher John Richter, "Fantasy rules over two-thirds of the universe, the past and the future, while reality is confined to the present. Fantasy—the original 'theater of the mind'—makes up a huge portion of human consciousness. Memory, as it filters through the mind's eye, is a kind of fantasy that gazes backward, into the past. Hope, anticipation, fear and ambition are fantasies that look toward the future."

Daydreaming allows your curious mind to explore your conscious mind in an unstructured way. It allows the space for you to explore various possibilities, and connect ideas that might not have been connected before, had you not given them time and space to connect.

Turns out there's a scientific reason for this. Daydreaming is an act of "non-directed thinking", which causes the front and the back of the brain to communicate – something that doesn't normally happen. It's a sign of an active brain and can improve memory, empathy, self-discovery and improve your mood. It seems our biological roots are saying

"OH hell NO" to societal views on daydreaming; it's reported that we spend 1/3 to 1/2 of our lives daydreaming. Take that society!

In November 2015, the Imagination Institute granted a research team with funds to research the link between daydreaming and creativity. The study, titled "The Benefits of Daydreaming for Creativity & Creative Writing", investigates "how daydreaming—a form of imaginative thought we all routinely engage in—affects creativity, and in particular creative writing. While daydreaming fills a substantial portion of our everyday life, and writers often report using their daydreams as a source of inspiration, very little is known about the kinds of daydreaming that are conducive to creativity."[59] Their goal was to develop an intervention that uses deliberate practice of daydreaming to increase creativity among students and aspiring writers.

The role of imagination in learning

Remember when we were kids, and we pretended that the floor was lava, and the only way to get across a room was to leap across the room on top of the furniture, from coffee table, to end table, to rocking chair, to try and get to the next room safely without burning to a crisp? I can still remember the exhilaration I felt before I jumped from the coffee table to the ottoman, as the distance was just farther than I was absolutely confident that I could stick the landing. I did NOT want to die a fiery death for the love of God!

Kids are extraordinarily great at suspending their belief in reality, considering all the possibilities, even if they're unrealistic. According to Scientific American Mind, this is an important part of the way kids learn.[60] "When something extraordinary is happening in a story or game, kids pay closer attention. This not only adds to the appeal of an activity such as make-believe, it can also help children learn more from a given situation."

59 http://dailyhealthpost.com/5-surprising-health-benefits-of-daydreaming/
60 Scientific American Mind, March/April 2016 pg. 46

People who daydream
are more likely to have
empathy.

Daydreaming
can lower blood
pressure.

Mind-wandering
promotes creativity.

The Scientifically Proven

BENEFITS OF
DAYDREAMING

Daydreaming, like
nighttime dreaming,
consolidates learning.

$$a^2 + b^2 = c^2$$

A wandering mind
usually has a better
working memory.

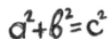

As humans, we never lose the ability to imagine. It is an important trait that we use to think critically about our environment to make informed decisions. "Thinking about unrealistic possibilities can help create informative contrasts with how reality does and does not work, bringing to light the structure of the real world," says Deena Weisberg, Psychology faculty member at the University of Pennsylvania. "Literature that takes place in fantastic landscapes can help us think deeply about our own world. And counterfactual history books can make us reconsider present circumstances by inviting us to reimagine our past."

AS HUMANS, WE NEVER LOSE THE ABILITY TO IMAGINE.

Just look at the top grossing genres in film. From 1995 to 2016, both comedy and adventure movies are tied at about 22% market share.[61] But interestingly, the number of adventure films produced is just 25% of that compared to the number of comedies made in the same time frame – 2,219 comedies versus 666 adventure films (coincidence, not the devil). Looking deeper at the top 25 grossing adventure films during the same time period, every single one contains an element of fantasy – magic, space, superheroes, aliens, fairies, talking toys, talking animals, monsters, trolls, ogres, and pirates. It seems that we just can't get enough of seeing unrealistic possibilities as a form of entertainment. What we don't realize, is that by opening up our minds to the fantastic, we are creating the societal guardrails that are necessary to figure out our own place in this world.

I have my own conspiracy theory about the relationship between Hollywood and the U.S. Government. I think it *could* be true that the Government has Hollywood make movies about scenarios they know are very possible – like aliens invading the earth spreading their outer space spores across the planet to wipe out the human race in an effort to steal

61 http://www.the-numbers.com/market/genre/Adventure

Top-Grossing Movies 1995-2016, Adjusted for Ticket Price Inflation

Rank	Movie	Release Date	Distributor	MPAA Rating	Total Gross	Inflation-Adjusted Gross
1	Star Wars Ep. VII: The Force Awakens	Dec 18, 2015	Walt Disney	PG-13	$932,318,187	$932,318,187
2	Star Wars Ep. I: The Phantom Menace	May 19, 1999	20th Century Fox	PG	$474,544,677	$761,329,663
3	The Avengers	May 4, 2012	Walt Disney	PG-13	$623,279,547	$660,081,224
4	Shrek 2	May 19, 2004	Dreamworks SKG	PG	$436,471,036	$592,504,152
5	Spider-Man	May 3, 2002	Sony Pictures	PG-13	$403,706,375	$585,756,409
6	Independence Day	Jul 2, 1996	20th Century Fox	PG-13	$306,124,059	$583,851,987
7	Pirates of the Caribbean: Dead Man's Chest	Jul 7, 2006	Walt Disney	PG-13	$423,315,812	$544,817,142
8	The Lord of the Rings: The Return of the King	Dec 17, 2003	New Line	PG-13	$377,845,905	$524,448,846
9	Finding Nemo	May 30, 2003	Walt Disney	G	$380,529,370	$518,148,559
10	Spider-Man 2	Jun 30, 2004	Sony Pictures	PG-13	$373,524,485	$507,054,974
11	Star Wars Ep. III: Revenge of the Sith	May 19, 2005	20th Century Fox	PG-13	$380,270,577	$500,106,226
12	The Lord of the Rings: The Two Towers	Dec 18, 2002	New Line	PG-13	$342,548,984	$492,516,107
13	Harry Potter and the Sorcerer's Stone	Nov 16, 2001	Warner Bros.	PG	$317,575,550	$472,336,516
14	The Lord of the Rings: The Fellowship of the Ring	Dec 19, 2001	New Line	PG-13	$315,544,750	$465,453,885
15	Men in Black	Jul 1, 1997	Sony Pictures	PG-13	$250,147,615	$459,419,843
16	Toy Story 3	Jun 18, 2010	Walt Disney	G	$415,004,880	$443,408,255
17	The Hunger Games: Catching Fire	Nov 22, 2013	Lionsgate	PG-13	$424,668,047	$440,249,458
18	Star Wars Ep. II: Attack of the Clones	May 16, 2002	20th Century Fox	PG	$302,181,125	$438,448,684
19	Pirates of the Caribbean: The Curse of the Black Pearl	Jul 9, 2003	Walt Disney	PG-13	$305,411,224	$426,967,926
20	Monsters, Inc.	Nov 2, 2001	Walt Disney	G	$289,423,425	$416,073,179
21	Frozen	Nov 22, 2013	Walt Disney	PG	$400,738,009	$414,997,174
22	Spider-Man 3	May 4, 2007	Sony Pictures	PG-13	$336,530,303	$412,347,448
23	Harry Potter and the Deathly Hallows: Part II	Jul 15, 2011	Warner Bros.	PG-13	$381,011,219	$405,034,625
24	Toy Story 2	Nov 19, 1999	Walt Disney	G	$245,823,397	$404,402,670
25	Shrek	May 18, 2001	Dreamworks SKG	PG	$267,655,011	$398,645,183

Complete List

our resources they've exhausted on their own highly evolved planet – just to prepare our lizard brains in the off off chance it *might* happen. This way, the Government can gauge sentiment and reactions of the general public about the movie against possible scenarios in their own efforts to prepare how to manage widespread worldwide panic and mayhem when the spore aliens actually arrive in real life.

If I disappear mysteriously when this book comes out, you all know why now. #justsayin

This time, you be the robot

The correlation of imagination and fantasy to sex is a no brainer. But I was curious as to why? If human beings have a physical need to connect and to procreate, why would we need to fantasize at all?

According to a study conducted at the University of Granada[62], sexual fantasies play a critical role in creating positive sexual desire, which is necessary to lead to excitation and orgasm. The study reports that having intercourse without desire may negatively affect the stages of sexual response. "Sexual desire is explained by a three-dimensional model, which includes social, psychological, and neurophysiologic aspects. For that reason, proper neurohormonal activity with a right sexual stimulation is necessary in order to experience sexual desire." In non-sciency terms, I think what they are trying to say is that positive sexual fantasies reduce anxiety, and make the getting it on part, way more ON than OFF.

So what do you think the top sexual fantasies are?

Turns out they're a little different for men and women.

"Women's private thoughts are much more creative and original than I could have

62 University of Granada. "Study Confirms Importance Of Sexual Fantasies In Experience Of Sexual Desire." ScienceDaily. ScienceDaily, 28 June 2007. www.sciencedaily.com/releases/2007/06/070627223851.htm

guessed," says Wendy Maltz, a nationally recognized Sex Therapist from Eugene, Oregon. "Also, I discovered that we can learn so much from our own fantasies. By consciously looking at our fantasy life, we can see how our erotic imagination has been shaped by personal life experiences and also by the larger culture. Then, we can use the power of our own minds to change fantasies we don't like and create new ones that turn us on in ways we truly enjoy."[63]

"The most common men's sexual fantasies are about your partners doing things they wouldn't ordinarily do," said sex researcher Pepper Schwartz, PhD, a sociology professor at the University of Washington in Seattle and co-author of "The Normal Bar." Schwartz said homosexual or bisexual men might have more freedom to play in this arena. "Gay men have a much broader palate," she said. "There is a gay culture that supports sexual fantasy. Dressing in drag or in costume and being willing to play different roles can lead to some exciting outcomes."

Anecdotally, I found it amusing that many of the sites I found with these Top 10 lists were a variation on "Health" or "Healthy". I am not sure what this means, perhaps a commentary on our skepticism to trust any content coming from a porn, kinky or fetish site, which is ironic as I would think THEY would be the experts on what people fantasize about, because it's their business to know exactly what will sell. #anotherthingtoponder

Turn the page for the Top 10 Sexual Fantasies for Men and Women. #TurnthePageNOW

TOP 10 WOMEN'S FANTASIES

10. BEAUTIFUL STRANGER ONE-NIGHT STAND

9. GROUP SEX

8. BEING A DOMINATRIX

7. HAVING AN AUDIENCE

6. BEING RAVAGED

5. BEING WITH A WOMAN WHILE
   THEIR MAN WATCHED

4. BEING A STRIPPER/ESCORT

3. THREESOME WITH TWO MEN

2. HAVING A STRAP-ON PENIS WITH THEIR PARTNER

1. BRADLEY COOPER*

*JUST KIDDING. IT'S PUBLIC SEX WITH A BAD BOY.

TOP 10 MEN'S FANTASIES

10. ROLE PLAY

9. FETISHES

8. DOMINATING THEIR PARTNER (BONDAGE)

7. HAVING SEX IN A PUBLIC PLACE

6. BEING TIED UP AND SPANKED

5. WATCHING THEIR PARTNER WITH ANOTHER PARTNER OF EITHER GENDER

4. ANAL SEX

3. THREESOME WITH TWO WOMEN

2. ORAL SEX

1. BEING DOMINATED*

* BY BRADLEY COOPER. JUST KIDDING. BUT SERIOUSLY, HE IS ONE TALL DRINK OF WATER.

Source: http://www.everydayhealth.com/mens-health-pictures/top-sexual-fantasies-for-men.aspx#01

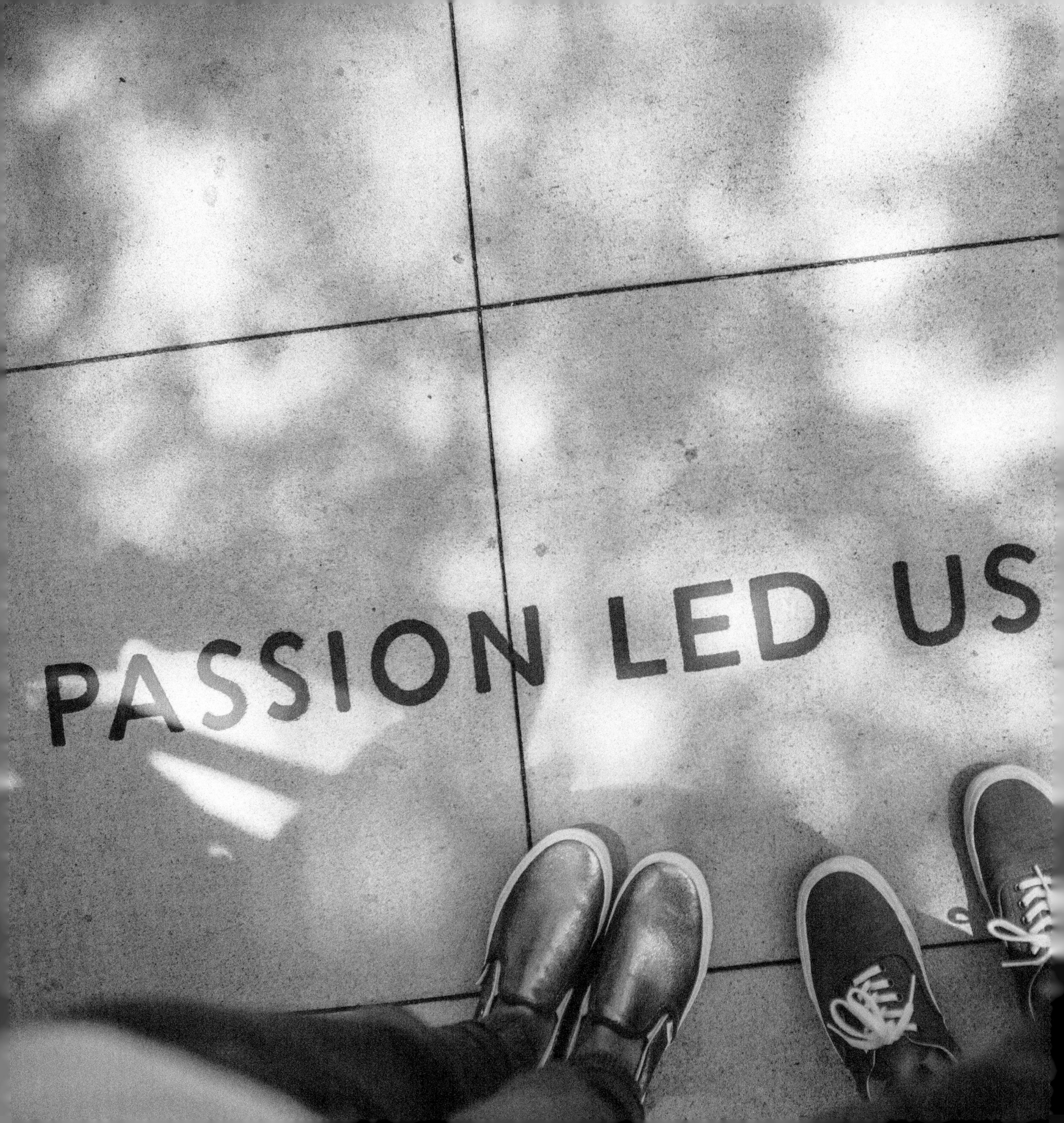
PASSION LED US

GET BEHIND SOMEONE

Why championing others can make a real difference

It takes guts to champion ideas, and people are no different. It's because championing someone requires investing yourself into who they are, what they can do, and putting your reputation on the line to stand up and say "Hey! I believe in you."

I think a great exercise for everyone to do is to think back about the people who have championed you in your life. Everyone has them. And every time someone does, it leads to the next chapter in your story.

Here's a short history of my champions: In 1987, my high school art teacher Bruce Rae, awarded me with "Senior Artist of the Year." I was not expecting it, as I never identified with being an "artist". I was a jock, lettering in four Varsity sports, who happened to like to draw. I asked him why he chose me over all the other seemingly more skilled students in the class. He said that he picked me yes, because of my talent, but more so because of my ability to listen to others and take direction, and apply the feedback to make my work better. He said this was the trait that would make me a great artist someday.

That advice, and my love for the arts, gave me the direction to major in Advertising and Graphic Design at Michigan State, and pursue a career as a designer.

This degree led to me to my first graphic design job in East Lansing, where a funny creativity AND sex story happened.

One of our clients was an outdoor company who needed help creating a billboard for their new client, an all-nude strip club called Déjà Vu Showgirls, which was founded in Lansing in 1978[66]. Their idea was to have a pair of women's legs hanging over the top of the billboard, so we decided to take a photo of my legs draped over a black board, to use as a template. This photo was then traced over as an illustration, and high heels and fishnet stockings were added for effect.

Well, as I understand it, that illustration became the logo for the club, and over the years, the business expanded. Today, they have 132 strip clubs in 36 U.S. states, the U.K., Australia, France, Canada and Mexico – and yes, I'm pretty sure those are still my legs. #Mylegsarefamous #Pleasedon'tbemyclaimtofame

It was at this job where I met Kirk MacKeller, who owned a print shop and was on the board of the Lansing American Advertising Federation's (AAF) Club. One day, he asked me to help design the materials for the ADDY Awards (Advertising creative competition), which led to a new design job and a seat on the board myself.

My rise in AAF leadership led me to the AAF National Conference in Washington DC in 1999, where I first met Bryan, who at the time was the incoming Vice President for his local San Jose Ad Club. We dated for two years long-distance before marrying in 2001, and are still partners and best friends with benefits in our consultancy, PureMatter.

It also led me to meet Erik Lohmeier, who served as AAF Western Region Chairman. Erik lives in Albuquerque, and in 2011, he owned an agency housed a floor above a movie production house. I was invited to judge the Albuquerque ADDYs that year, and as part

66 https://en.wikipedia.org/wiki/D%C3%A9j%C3%A0_Vu_(company)

THE MOST CREATIVE LICENSE EVER TAKEN ON
ANY LOGO IN THE HISTORY OF THE UNIVERSE

of the experience, I had to give a short presentation about "anything" to their Ad Club the night before the event. **What the H.** I am squeamish enough about presenting to large crowds, and now I was expected to talk about something interesting to a group of my industry peers?! Fuuuuuuuc.....

Serendipity took care of me, as this is where the idea for "Creativity is Like Sex" was first born, conceived appropriately in the shower (as you would expect), arriving with such brute force I still swear it was supernaturally planted there. This idea turned into a presentation titled "The 10 Reasons Why Creativity is Like Sex", and I gave it for the first time in the ballroom at the Hotel Albuquerque to about 150 very confused peers and students. #TWSS

When I was done, they didn't know whether to laugh or applaud, so I got the <slow clap> – which I take today as an indicator that I was onto something.

A few days later, I had lunch with Erik, and we talked about the presentation, as he had already heard about it from his movie producer building mate. Apparently, this guy thought it was funny and flippantly mentioned to Erik that he thought it would make a great movie. As we talked, Erik agreed with the idea, and encouraged me to consider writing a screenplay about it. I thought he was smoking crack. Yes, I am a writer, but I had never considered writing a movie and didn't know the first thing about it. I have, as you now know, always been enamored with Hollywood and movies, so I figured, why the hell not give it a try?

I started storyblocking my outline in a Word doc, and when that became unmanageable to track my thoughts and the story, I bought some screenplay software. This made it much easier to format, which allowed me to focus on the story and characters. Then I blocked off time each week to write some pages, and nine months later, I had literally birthed my first screenplay, titled "Mojo".

It was one of the proudest moments of my life. I pushed my boundaries and did something I never knew I could do, and this accomplishment ranks in my top five life achievements. (Now, I never said it was great – remember that practice, perspective and persistence thing?! But it got done.)

The process of writing my screenplay reinvigorated my creative spirit, because I felt like I championed myself – something not many people talk about. I challenged my writing skills in a new direction, and for the first time, felt that "autolectic" feeling that I felt again while writing this book. It feels super great to prioritize doing the things you love; even better when you actually do them. I believe that's what we were put on this earth to fulfill.

None of this would have happened had these people not championed my ideas, talents, or capabilities.

Who could you be a champion for? How could it enrich their life?

That time BK spoke at TED

One of the greatest examples of getting behind someone is when Bryan (or BK as we call him) was invited to give a TED talk. I am sure you're familiar with TED.com – it stands for "Technology, Entertainment and Design" – and in my opinion, is one of the greatest brain trusts of human information of all time. (I *really* hope the aliens find that website first before they find TMZ.)

When you get invited to give a TED talk, you're assigned a curator to coach you through the process. Bryan was lucky enough to get Juliet Blake, a big Hollywood producer who has worked with Jim Henson, and recently partnered with Oprah and Steven Spielberg to bring the Helen Mirren movie "The Hundred Foot Journey" to the big screen.

The time Juliet invested in helping Bryan succeed was impressive. She took his calls when he had a question. She helped him understand the process, the cadence of a great talk, where to draw inspiration from, and how to be a great storyteller. She was also the one, who at 7:30pm the night before Bryan's talk, ripped up his script and said "I like it better when you're just speaking from your heart. Do that, and you'll be great." #HolyMaaloxMoment

ACHIEVING YOUR GOALS REQUIRES THE UNDENIABLE, UNSHAKABLE BELIEF IN WHAT YOU'RE DOING.

And he did! (Watch it please, search Bryan Kramer on TED.com). The over 300 hours he spent trying to memorize his talk paid off, and he rose to the challenge – just like I knew he would. That experience made both of us grow – a lot – and being championed by Juliet helped both of us get there.

Trusting your passion

The one commonality I've seen in people who achieve a personal goal is one that can't be faked, no matter how hard they try. It's the undeniable, unshakable belief in what they're doing.

What's the saying? If you want to get what you want, act like you own the place. It takes guts, focus, and moxie to conquer the hard stuff in life.

Well, it's one thing to believe in what you're doing. But convincing yourself that what you believe is worth redirecting your entire life for, that's a huge hurdle.

The beauty of Cherin Choi

Sometimes, remembering what excites you takes some soul searching, and getting out of your own way is the only way to get there. I connected with Cherin Choi, LA "colorist to the stars", through our profile similarities on Red Bull's "Hacking Creativity"[67] website experiment . I was curious to hear her perspective on creativity since our profiles were a match, but our career paths were so different.

She explained to me her journey.

> I used to have a corporate job that I really wasn't very happy at, but I was very good at it. And I didn't know if I should keep going or what to do, and this caused me to have a "quarter-life crisis." I decided to go travel and find myself like an "Eat, Pray, Love" kind of thing.
>
> Once I finished my trip, I remembered that I wanted to go to beauty school when I was in high school, and I decided to check it out. It just fit all the things that I saw myself doing when I was younger. And when I moved back to Los Angeles five years ago, I just did. I said, "I'm going to beauty school and see how I like it and do hair" and that was it, to be honest. That's the honest truth.

She makes it sound simple, but I am sure there were plenty of soul searching, agonizing moments during her decision-making process that could have derailed her following her true passion. We all face those moments daily, weekly, monthly – our whole lives. It is exhausting being committed, focused and passionate. But the irony of it all is if you try to evade what your heart wants, the deeper a hole it bores into your psyche, and it will not be ignored.

I was so happy to hear Cherin mention her "Quarter-life crisis", which I also talked about with Caroline Beaton. I didn't know it was a "thing" until I started researching this book. "While mid- and late- life crises are often triggered by important life events, such as health problems, widowhood, retirement, divorce or job loss, quarter-life crises often lack provocation," Caroline says. "Our career is chugging along per usual when a simple question falls from the sky and shatters our okay routine: "Is this it?"

TONY ROBBINS WISDOM BOMB –>
CHANGE HAPPENS IN AN INSTANT; IT'S
DECIDING TO CHANGE THAT TAKES FOREVER.

I went through one too. I spent a few lost years searching for my identity post college, newly married to my first husband and trying to find my foothold in my world – there were times I thought I didn't have the strength to make it through. I remember hitting rock bottom at about age 26, as I caught a glimpse of myself in my bathroom mirror and was startled to not recognize the face staring back at me. I realized in that moment, that I had veered so far off my life's course that I couldn't see any of myself in my reflection. I knew I had two choices – to live, or to die. I made a choice to live that day, and decided to take life minute by minute, until I could take it hour by hour, until I could take it day by day.

As Tony Robbins says, change happens in an instant; it's deciding to change that takes forever. If I have any advice for Millennials out there struggling with the same feelings, it's that you're no different than any Gen Xer or Boomer out there. You're human, and

just like generations who have gone before us, you have your own, but different set of problems and plagues to figure out. Everyone struggles with identity at some point in their lives, and it happens as a course correction to get us back on our path to become who we're supposed to be, so we can contribute the very best of us to our time on Earth.

Sometimes, it needs to be bigger

I've worked really hard in my life, as each year passes, to not become hardened and jaded about people's motivations in business. I get that we're all in business for a reason. We have to make money and provide for our families and fuel the economy and blah de blah. But remember those days, like back when we were in grade school, when we used to start every sentence with "Pretend that…", which sparked your friends to add something else to the game. As adults, how do we keep that spirit alive to eek out every bit of fun and delight in our 12-14 hour days? I know most of my best ideas start with the words "Oh!! Wouldn't it be cool if…". Why the hell can't I just start there and be able to run with it??

The experience of taking my idea about the ways creativity is like sex from a PowerPoint presentation, to a screenplay, to now a book, taught me that sometimes, ideas need to shape shift. Just because my screenplay hasn't sold yet doesn't mean it won't, but maybe it's just not ready. Maybe it's really, really sucky and the Universe has done me a massive favor. Maybe a movie isn't the way my message is wanting to be released into the world.

I have learned that the reason to do it is to focus on the message, not the medium (which is SO effing ironic because in my job, we tell clients that all the time. Why don't I listen to myself more?! #thestruggleisreal). I have learned that for me, if my heart isn't in it, I can't be a part of it, because emptiness and being trite (triticity?) just isn't my thing. Just don't be afraid to shapeshift and share your big ideas, because they'll eventually find their way into the world. They are tenacious as F-U-C-K.

Use your mouth more often

When you share parts of yourself with others, it gives you both a new perspective. I had an incredible business coach for about 6 months, who has since become a dear friend named Jane Finette. She helped me stay on track with the writing of this book, and reminded me that what I had to contribute to

IT TAKES 2 SECONDS TO TELL SOMEONE "YOU'RE DOING A GREAT JOB!!!!"

this world was exactly right and perfect for me. I also got to learn about her incredible non-profit called The Coaches Fellowship, which provides pro bono leadership training to women who would otherwise never be able to receive it because of a lack of financial, cultural or any other resources to do so. I found her work so inspiring, and she found my work inspiring. Our 6 months of coaching was an experience that gave me a new perspective about the worth of what I was doing with my talents, and raised my awareness about the necessary and meaningful work Jane is contributing to the world.

What a great reminder that you can exercise your creativity by helping someone else be creative. It literally charges your batteries, and it works both ways. It can be as simple as taking the time to recognize the efforts of someone you respect and admire. Seriously, it takes 2 seconds to tell someone "you're doing a great job!!!!" people! This acknowledgement can be just the remedy to keep them moving toward their purpose.

It's why I'm writing this book, because one person can make a difference.

So why not you?

Save your space
Cycle right
Right the cycle
Simply Stored
Space your personal frontier
Freedom spot
Embrace your space
FrEE (expired electronics)
Give it back
What's your space plan?
Give it back for good
Safe Dump
Ewaste less
Energize your environment
Dispose Right Network
Space station
Give it a proper burial
Drop off for good.
Electronic after life
Ignore no more
Happy ending
Ewaste Less
Ewaste Deficit Plan
Lay it to rest
Drop Spot
Go neutral
Device life
The Planet Plan
BE the plan
My ewaste Plan
Right Recycle
Release it!
Waste free future
Plan E
replace at e-place
replace displace clean space eplace
Drop stop
Mean it when you clean it
Waste space
power your space power your future
Clutter core
Use your space for good
Electronics - we're so wasted!
ecycle your world
Re-energize your electronics
Plug into your personal space
Ewaste takes up space
Mine your closet
Plug Purgatory

GO DEEPER

Going past the first idea.

We talked about the inclination of all of us sometimes just wanting to stop and move on when you think you have a great idea.

But what happens when you do go past the first idea? What magic is unlocked when you go back to your research, sticky notes and papers, and look for new connections that create a deeper, more meaningful connection to the story you're trying to tell?

In his thought-provoking presentation called "Exploiting Chaos", Jeremy Gutche, CEO and founder of Trendhunter, shares a great breakdown about the ideation process that Austin-based agency GSD&M applied when the state of Texas asked them to help solve their state's rampant littering problem.

He explains that when you become obsessed with your audience – not just their functional behaviors, motivations, and emotional connections to the issue/product/solution at hand, but most importantly understand the cultural connection to why, and how they fit into that story – you can find the magic.

GSD&M was obsessed with their littering audience. As you would suspect, the likely suspects were young males 18-30, who drove pick up trucks with gun racks and drank beer. But the cultural connection they discovered this audience shared was a "King of my World" lifestyle that connected them together. Their creative solution was to enlist a few Texans already viewed as sources of pride to this audience, Dallas Cowboys players Randy White and Ed "Too-Tall" Jones, with this message: "Don't mess with Texas."

This now infamous TV spot first ran in 1987, and in just three years by 1990, litter in Texas had decreased a whopping 72%. The campaign is still going today with other famous Texans like Willie Nelson and George Strait, and the "Don't Mess with Texas" moniker is now culturally synonymous with the state.

Understanding where people fit into the story is what makes ideas stick.

There's a famous story that John Lasseter, Chief Creative Officer of Pixar Animation Studios, tells about his close friend, Steve Jobs. He said that they were having dinner together the night before the 1995 debut of Pixar's first movie, Toy Story, and Steve revealed to John that he was going to take the company public. John recalled the pressure he felt when he heard that, but then Steve said to him, "At Apple, the lifespan of the computers I make is about 3 years, 5 years max, but then it's a doorstopper. What you do, if you do your job well, your stories will last forever." John recalled that he had never thought about it like that before, and it made him feel better about what he was doing.

Little did I know that Steve Jobs' doorstoppers, and Jeremy Gutche's ideation approach would together lead to the creation of one of the most successful campaigns of my career.

eCollective: Take it back for good™

PureMatter was approached by ECS Refining to help bring to life a consumer electronic-waste (e-waste) collection pilot program for the state of California. This concept was the brainchild of Carey Baker, who was, at the time their Marketing Manager (and side note: ironically, I learned that Carey and Jane Finette are friends and colleagues as business coaches today #whatarethechances #smallworld). She envisioned that there was a way to do good work and raise awareness about ECS being the only truly responsible e-waste recycler in the United States. Yes, you read that right – ECS is the only e-waste recycler who reclaims the precious materials in e-waste domestically, then recycles the rest, never shipping anything oversees or dumping it into landfills. This is not a shameless plug; they are not a client anymore, just doing their part to save the planet no big deal.

At this time in 2010, the cultural perception was that electronic waste was a nuisance to personal space and for the environment, but in the spectrum of annoyance versus action, recycling it was a low priority. Those old cell phones and TVs were fine sitting in their basements and storage units, and could be dealt with later. Or, if they were recycled, it was easy enough to just take them to Goodwill or a church recycling drive for someone else to deal with.

But in reality, this e-waste clutter is an ever-growing health and environmental issue with real ramifications. Old electronics contain lead, zinc, magnesium, acid, silver and gold, as well as hundreds of other precious metals, toxic plastics and chemicals. When burned in landfills, the smoke can cause cancer. When it's shipped overseas, not only does much of it end up in the ocean poisoning the sea life, but also in massive piles in China where it's pillaged for precious metals and illegally burned. One small town in China near an e-waste heap was found to have over 90% of its children suffering from lead poisoning as a direct result of the incessant burning they were breathing and drinking from their water source.

In 2010, every man, woman and child on the planet produced 12 pounds of e-waste a year. This is shocking to hear – but unfortunately, not enough to make people go clean out their closets to responsibly recycle their old electronics.

This only frames the problem, which is not enough to inspire action. We needed to understand who these people were in California who would be motivated enough to recycle their e-waste at an eCollective™ location (the name and brand developed for the program). After building our personas of three likely audiences, we focused on "Laura", a married woman in her early 40s, with kids and a full time job. Laura is concerned with the overall health and safety of her home and thinks it would be great to get the electronic waste in her garage and closet out of the house, but her family is not motivated to recycle, and lifting a large old TV into her car on her own is not practical. She is also not sure where to take them, so they just stay put in her home. She's a little murky on the whole "green" movement too. All of this information helped us better understand "Laura", but what was the cultural connection she had to the issue?

Using Jeremy Gutche's methodology, we did a deeper analysis of our initial categorizations, and spotted a second set of common themes that became descriptive of the attitudes about why this group would or wouldn't recycle their e-waste.

Each attitude was given a descriptor:

1. **Skeptisociety:** As a group, there was skepticism about corporate motivations to require constant upgrades, planned obsolescence and new products.

2. **Ignorewareness:** The attitudes of the group reflected a good-intentioned ignorance fueled by lack of awareness about the issues surrounding storing e-waste in your home, and around your family.

3. **Emotronics:** People have a real emotional connection to their electronics.

4. **Intention-ease-tas:** People intend to do the right thing but it has to be easy for them to implement.

5. **Jonesingers:** People are enamored with having the latest, greatest gadget – "keeping up with the Joneses" – and want to tell everyone about it.

Knowing how Laura identified culturally into the issue helped us understand her world – that she really did want to do the right thing, but she needed to also benefit directly from her actions so she could feel great about her choice.

This led us to our campaign slogan: "Take it back for good", which told her that she was not only doing the right thing, but recycling her e-waste would help de-clutter her life, for good. The safe, easy and free part was the payoff.

By the time the program launched, there was an eCollective location within 5 miles of 90% of households in California (if you live in California, visit www.myecollective.com and find one in your neighborhood.) It's now the most successful electronic take back program in California history.

[I would add in a #micdrop but *technically a microphone is considered e-waste and that has no place on the ground.]

Using feedback to make your work better

For a long time after I wrote my screenplay, I didn't want anyone to read it. I was so proud of completing it, that I was fearful that no one else would feel the same way about it. Stephen Pressfield, author of many books including *The Legend of Bagger Vance*,

The War of Art and *Do the Work*, calls that being an "amateur" in your craft – and that perfectly describes how I was feeling about my own work. I had not considered anything other than myself when it came to my screenplay, so much so, that it prevented me from making it better.

Years later, after starting and abandoning another screenplay halfway through, I revisited my original work,

FEEDBACK HELPS YOU GET OUT OF YOUR OWN HEAD. IT MAKES YOUR WORK BETTER – EVEN IF YOU DON'T AGREE WITH IT.

and realized I wanted to return my focus on making it come to life. I became a member of Stage32.com, a really cool online community for people aspiring to be in the film and TV business, and started submitting my logline (the 1-2 sentence description that is supposed to summarize your film) and my pitch (the longer 1-page version of a logline) into their weekly producer reviews. These reviews offer, for a small fee, the chance to get feedback from people in the film industry who review your work, then return back a critique and score from 1-5 about what you submit.

At first, hearing any criticism made me feel insecure and defensive. But it also made me go back and make tweaks. As more feedback came in, I started to see patterns, which helped me focus on the specific areas that really needed to be worked on. I made it my goal to get someone to request to read my full-length script off my written pitch – and after four months of working, tweaking, and resubmitting, I finally got a request from a major production company to read my script. OH MY GOD IT HAPPENED.

I was over the moon, that was, until the feedback came back from the producer who read my script, returned with a big fat "PASS". "The characters are unlikeable", she said. "And you need to go back and correct the formatting, because it's not industry-standard." #FML

WHA-PSSHHH. The feedback slapped me right across the face. But it also made me remember that in focusing on making my pitch better, I had not yet gone back to work on the script itself. I went back and re-read it, and she was right. There is more work to do there.

There is always more work to do.

Going past your first impression.

So what about the sex part, you ask?

Just remember that you don't always have the full story and should never jump to conclusions until you have enough perspective to realize what you're really looking at.

TOO CLOSE

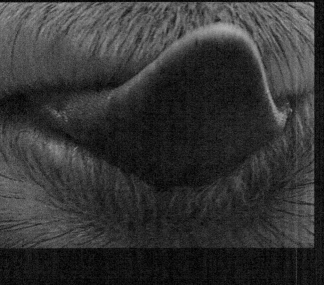

MUCH BETTER

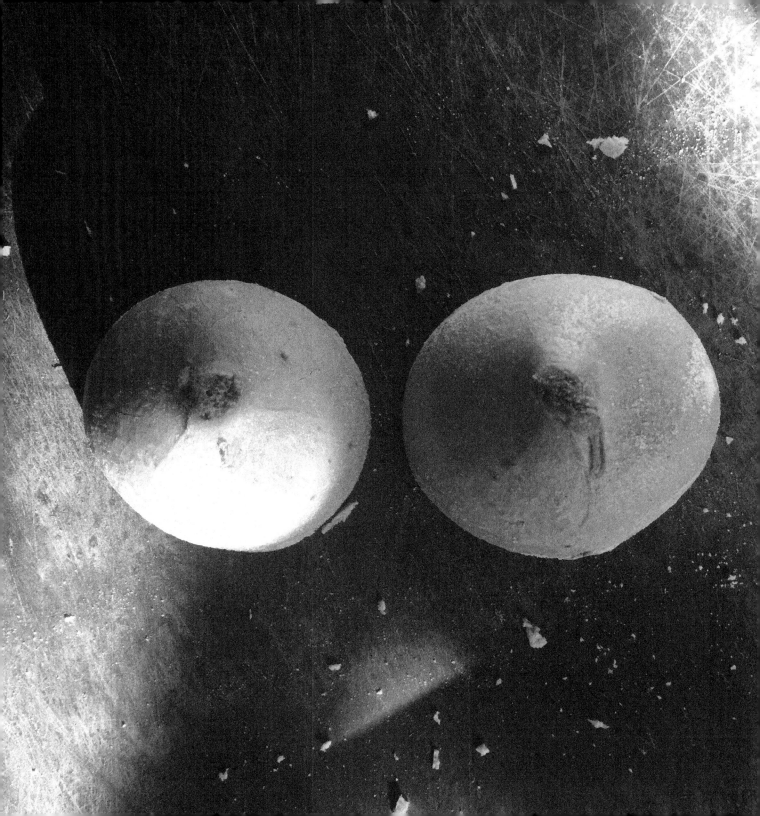

EMBRACE TITS:
THINK IT THROUGH, SERIOUSLY

Start with the end in mind

We all have stories about a project we've been involved in, or an endeavor we've started with enthusiasm and vigor, only to have it fall flat on its face somewhere along the way. We stand around, scratching our bruised heads, trying to figure out where things went sideways to see if it could be righted. And, it seems no matter how hard we try to make it work, each time we try, it loses a little more energy until we all can't remember why we wanted to do it in the first place.

These projects all lack TITS: Thinking It Through Seriously. A lack of TITS is the inventor of the face palm.

TITS should be the thing you tack onto the end of your sentences when you think of an idea, like the Chinese fortune cookie game "between the sheets." You know, whatever your fortune is – "You will prosper and be showered with affection" – you add "between the sheets" to the end.

"I think I want to remodel the kitchen" turns into "I think I want to remodel the kitchen but TITS first."

The simple addition of this acronym to our ideas actually changes the outcomes of the effort. It's true. Because when we don't think things through, seriously, we are unable to consider potential roadblocks that could have been prevented that yes, deliver us valuable learning and insight, but can also be costly and time consuming.

TITS cannot be avoided.

Get inside the box

Putting your creativity to task is where process is the champion. Creativity is always better when supported by strategy, planning and management behind it. To many people, this seems contrary to what they've been told, in that creativity is this free, unstructured activity where the mind is allowed to go where it goes to find new connections. This is true – kinda true. Half true. Think of creativity as this tornadic-like vortex spinning in your head. It is powerful, and picks up speed as it lifts debris in its path. It's unpredictable, and can very easily get off track and out of control if not contained within a finite space.

Imagine a clear malleable box around this vortex, that keeps the energy of the tornado intact but also keeps it from spinning away too far in any direction, or from destroying anything. This malleable box is the process, the structured approach that can be infinitely repeated to produce infinite outcomes.

These guardrails help team members focus their best thinking. This is especially true if your business depends on innovation. In the words of Harvard Business Review, "When you're in an Innovation Community, where participation is open and governance is flat, process is the best enabler to bring people together more quickly and achieve a common goal."

A flat governance culture supports the belief that great ideas can come from anyone.

And this can actually happen as a repeatable process, when everyone understands where you're starting, and where you want to end up. This creates a complex challenge, as opposed to a complicated one. Complex challenges are never open-ended or fuzzy from the start. It's like planning a road trip; when you know where you are, and where you're going, you still have infinite possibilities of ways to get there. Do you prefer to sightsee? Maybe taking scenic back roads is the best way to go. Do you need to get there quickly? I'd recommend an airplane instead of driving, which could be more expensive but the fastest route. When you know the end goal, and where you're starting, you can prioritize the best possible route or strategy to meet your goals.

CREATIVITY TAKES INSPIRATION.

PROCESS TAKES DEDICATION.

So the next time you hear someone say "Think outside the box!" you can turn to them and say "NO! I am TITS deep INSIDE the box!" Not only will you enjoy their reaction, you will get better ideas. #winwin #yourewelcome

And what about the other famous idiom "If at first you don't succeed, try, try again." Yes, of course, don't ever stop trying #twss But take your TITS with you, and you might find yourself without so many bruises. Sometimes you think you're TITS but you're really only TIT and this is where lessons are learned. We're all human, and mistakes will happen, so if things don't turn out how you thought they would, just reset, learn and start over. So, pretty much just read the first sentence of this paragraph again. #10secondsyoullnevergetback

Sometimes, it sucks

Everyone wants to feel like they understand the beginning, middle and end of a story. And when communicating an idea to others, it's TITS that communicators really need if they want any of their coolest, weirdest or crazy ideas to stand a chance of surviving against a sea of villagers holding pitchforks and torches ready to turn against it. This requires thoughtful storytelling, so the audience has the context they need to understand why one idea may be more risky, but probably way better than another safer choice.

But sometimes, no amount of explaining will mitigate the feeling of risk. We work with large, Titanic-sized enterprise businesses, many (but not all) of them full of deep levels of political bureaucracy. Hand to God, sometimes I think it would be easier to survive in North Korea jumping up and down with a megaphone in a clown suit than it would be in some of these corporate departments. The backstabbing. Contradiction. The jockeying for favortism or promotions. I would survive exactly a day and half in that environment, and only because it would take me a full day to figure out which floor and cubicle was mine. Environments like this is where creativity goes to die.

In these fear-fueled environments, taking a risk on a new hardhitting concept seems way too scary and unconventional. This is why ideas that start out great eventually get watered down by layers of approvers, then legal, and end up looking exactly like what everyone else is doing, which makes everyone feel better but sells nothing and is forgotten before it hits the market.

To someone in the creative field, this consistent beating-down of ideas is a soul-sucking purgatory. Anyone reading this now who witnesses someone in your own company saying "Well, I personally like it but it's too risky," can I plead with you to please, in the name of all things sparkly, throw a stapler at their head?! This has been a public service announcement brought to you by TITS.

Get yourself a model

There is a chasm between over-thinking an idea, and thinking it through. Seriously. If I were to draw this as a model, imagine over-thinking ideas on the left, and thinking it through on the right.

$$(\bullet) (\bullet)$$

You see the chasm in the middle? I told you. #ThoughtCleavage

So what about TITS and sex?

Oh, come on, people. This is a pseudo-businessney book. If you can't make this connection, we've got bigger issues to tackle.

~ WORDS OF WISDOM ~

CONFUCIOUS SAYS THAT
FOR EVERY ADDITIONAL APPROVER ON
A PROJECT, YOU SHOULD ADD ANOTHER
ZERO TO YOUR INVOICE.

Coffee

data · date
titolo · title

autore · author

premi letterari · awards   Water

editore · publisher   Water

libreria · bookstore   Water

biblioteca · library

ho da · suggested by

commenti · comments

                            Wine Wine Wine Wine
                            Wine Wine Wine Wine
                            Wine Wine Wine Wine
                            Wine Wine Wine Wine
                            Wine

prestato a/da

DO IT EVERY DAY

The practice of rituals in creativity

All of us, at some point in our lives, have practiced a routine of some sort to get us ready for an activity. Grabbing a cup of coffee before settling down to check email in the morning. Or doing that last minute "teeth check" in the mirror by your front door just to make sure there's no food stuck in between.

When these routines are practiced consistently, they become habits and can be performed on an unconscious level where we go into autopilot, not even realizing we do them anymore.

So what's the difference between a routine and a ritual? This question intrigued me, because for me, routine equals safety and security but also boredom and low energy. I will never produce my most creative outputs if the inputs don't excite or challenge me. But I also perform a series of consistent activities to prepare me for the headspace I need to write. I do them routinely, but they don't feel boring or mundane to me – and so I learned that that's precisely the difference between a routine and a ritual.

A routine is something that is disconnected from the narrative of your day, is dutiful and task-driven, and relatively meaningless.

A ritual is highly connected to your internal narrative, has meaning and purpose, and is performed as a positive action aware of the outcome you envision.

The coolest part is that by being more aware of your desired outcome in any activity you perform throughout the day, you can use a ritualistic-approach to assign more meaning to what you're doing. Getting dressed in the morning can go from an annoyance, to an act of purpose if framed not as just getting dressed, but as something you are doing to contribute to your higher desire to be perceived as being confident and professional. Steven Handle[68] described it like this. "Instead of feeling like every daily activity is something that 'just needs to get done,' it becomes an activity you feel serves a positive function in your life, and it becomes something you may even enjoy doing and look forward to. Ultimately, the more meaning you can add to your daily activities, the more motivated you become to do them."

It turns out you can practice creativity as a habitual behavior, according to psychologist Robert Epstein, PhD, author of "The Big Book of Creativity Games" (McGraw-Hill, 2000). When you can strike a nice balance of establishing connections with other people, things, activities, ideas, experiences and stories, it forces us to get out of our own routine. Creating these new connections is like brainfood. It's why everyone should take at least 2 vacations a year. And go on Sabbatical. And go for walks. And try new foods (even if they look gross or have anything to do with seafood – Ok I lied, I'm not eating any organs or half alive body parts or anything black or weirdly textured that comes out of the ocean. I'm drawing the line there, people.) But and, and, and, you get it. You really do have to force yourself out of your routines and move them into the habitually ritualistic category on purpose. When you can do this, something magical happens.

68 http://www.theemotionmachine.com/routines-vs-rituals
69 http://www.apa.org/gradpsych/2009/01/creativity.aspx

Despite the widely held belief that some people just aren't endowed with the creativity gene, "There's not really any evidence that one person is inherently more creative than another," Epstein says. "Instead, creativity is something that anyone can cultivate."[69] Preach it brutha!

"As strange as it sounds, creativity can become a habit," says creativity researcher Jonathan Plucker, PhD, a psychology professor at Indiana University. "Making it one helps you become more productive."

How to be ritual and famous

I thought it would be helpful and interesting to hear what rituals a few people you might recognize practiced.

Benjamin Franklin asked himself the same morning and evening questions, every day.[70] When he rose, he asked himself "What good shall I do this day?" and upon going to sleep, he asked "What good have I done today?" He also sat in his room completely naked for an hour in the cold, citing it made his bones hurt less and gave him the most restful nap afterwards. Ben doesn't even know he had stumbled upon the beginnings of cryotherapy – probably because dry ice was invented 50 years after his death. #soclose

CREATIVITY IS SOMETHING THAT ANYONE CAN CULTIVATE.

Barack Obama and Steve Jobs have something in common as well. They both believe(d) in minimizing mundane distractions, like wearing the exact same thing every day to prevent decision fatigue. (Something my husband, Bryan also believes. Any of you who know him recognize the "BK Uniform" – a short-sleeved black shirt, dark jeans and black shoes).

Decision fatigue – is that really a thing? According to Wikipedia[71], it is. "In decision making and psychology, decision fatigue refers to the deteriorating quality of decisions made by an individual, after a long session of decision making. It is now understood as one of the causes of irrational trade-offs in decision making. For instance, judges in court have been shown to make less favorable decisions later in the day than early in the day. Decision fatigue may also lead to consumers making poor choices with their purchases."

It goes on to say, "There is a paradox in that 'people who lack choices seem to want them and often will fight for them"; yet at the same time, 'people find that making many choices can be [psychologically] aversive." OK, two comments here... 1) Never partake in a long session of decision making #ew #soundskinky and 2) What exactly is the right amount of choices, why can't someone just tell me how many choices to give, I have kids and this information would be very helpful thank you the end.

Rituals for those in the creative arts take on a new level of importance. Stephen Pressfield has his daily mantra and ritual that he practices habitually every day before he starts writing. He developed these rituals to combat what he calls "The Resistance", which is present in each and every one of us. My business coach, Jane, calls it "The Saboteur" (Mine is named "Monsieur Non", he looks like Inigo Montoya from Princess Bride and Captain Hook had a baby, which is weird since they're both guys.) It's the force of resistance that is always trying to sabotage our own success.

We literally can't help ourselves from preventing our own success. It takes many forms – TV, friends, surfing the web, Facebook, housework – anything that takes us away from actually doing the work we were meant to do, but will do anything to avoid doing. Stephen knows that he needs to tackle Resistance first thing when he gets up. For him,

71 https://en.wikipedia.org/wiki/Decision_fatigue

Meet my Saboteur, Monsier Non. He is annoying.

that means getting out of the house and hitting the gym, every morning. And before he writes, he calls upon his muses, because he knows that true professionals understand they are merely a vessel for stories coming through from minds much smarter and evolved than our own egos. This is why creating a ritualistic space is so important for writers; to create the favorable conditions you need to hear these voices clearly. As he says, "if you are a real writer, you have no choice. You have to confront your talent or die."

It's an innie

That well-known saying about "creative outlets" is, in my opinion, missing the part of the story that helps explain how to make that experience fulfilling. People putting themselves in situations where they can express their best selves through doing what they love IS their creativity "outletting" itself. But also making the time and space to quiet your mind, think about the interesting connections in your life and listen to those voices shouting whispers of inspiration into your consciousness – this is your creative *inlet*. I believe you can't have one without the other.

For me, creating a sacred inlet to write is my ritual. When I started approaching my writing as a necessary part of my week, and scheduling it into my activities consistently every Sunday afternoon, my satisfaction and sense

IF YOU ARE A REAL WRITER, YOU HAVE NO CHOICE. YOU HAVE TO CONFRONT YOUR TALENT OR DIE. ~ STEPHEN PRESSFIELD

of accomplishment went way up. I feel like I am making a commitment to myself to carve out time just for me, in order to conjure what needs to be said and heard.

Our house isn't that big, but fortunately, my husband and kids all prefer Sunday afternoons to themselves, doing their own projects in their own rooms. All I need is a 4-hour chunk of time, my Spotify, wifi and my laptop, and I am good to go. And by setting these expectations with my family, they see how important it is to me and are OK with it. Nothing has suffered – in fact, I would say our family lives have improved, because I am a happier person, which makes everyone happier. Our collective energy is more grounded, in large part because when you make time against your Saboteur to do what you love and feel drawn to create, your sense of purpose comes flooding in spades.

What do I do to silence my Msr. Non? I tell him he has a small penis. That pretty much shuts him up… at least for a while.

Speaking of penis

When you think about rituals and sex, for me it evokes a visual of that one scene in the movie "Eyes Wide Shut" – a bunch of naked people silently walking around a Baroque ballroom with Mardi Gras masks and long velvet capes. What does that even mean?!

But in the spirit of exploring a ritualistic approach to sex, meaning mindfully making it a part of a habitual experience, it turns out that adding rituals to your sex life can make you extraordinarily happy. According to bustle.com, people who have sex every day are more "creative, confident, and all-around awesome."[72] Since "awesome" is somewhat of an ambiguous descriptor, let's dig a little deeper.

"There have been lots of studies describing the health benefits of sex," says licensed sex therapist and sexuality educator Sandra L. Caron, PhD, professor of family relations and human sexuality at the University of Maine's College of Education and Human Development in Orono. "Most of them relate to achieving orgasm. Nobody says you have to be with someone to do that."

Whoa, Whoa, slow down. Wait a minute here. Asking for a friend now… she is specifically referring to the orgasm as having health benefits, whether you're with *any* number of people, including just yourself? It turns out that's true as well. Good news! People have feared going blind and buying razors to shave the hair off their palms all these years for NOTHING. #nowSchickgoesbankrupt #sellyourstock

So here are the scientifically researched and found to be true benefits of having an orgasm every day[73]:

- **It's great for your heart.** Not only does a daily orgasm lower your risk for heart attack and stroke, it also is the equivalent of walking 4-6 MPH. It's like a treadmill for your privates!

- **It eases pain.** Put down that bottle of Advil and get busy instead. Having an orgasm is shown to decrease feelings of pain and stress, including those Aunt Flo brings every month.

- **It makes you look younger.** That 'morning after' glow isn't just a term. Orgasms make your blood vessels open, making your face flush and possibly plumping up wrinkles on your face. Cheaper than face cream… I'll take it!

- **It improves your mood.** If I need to explain this one you're doing it wrong.

- **It prevents cancer.** OK, I am a little skeptical of this one, as my research found that studies suggest that orgasms reduce the chance of men getting Prostate Cancer because of the stimulation of testicles. #ewjustwantyourballstouched

73 http://www.everydayhealth.com/sexual-health/seven-healthy-reasons-to-have-sex-right-now.aspx

Deepak Chopra says #sorrynotsorry

Deepak Chopra said "Creativity is ultimately sexual – I'm sorry – but it is!" Well Deep, no need to be sorry, because here's some great news: According to National Geographic[74], researchers at the University of Newcastle correlated that daily sex boosts creativity! YEAH! But wait, there's more: Only if all that sex is being had with lots of different people. #Boooo #Monogamyweepseverywhere

The study found that poets and artists have twice as many sexual partners than those who are not engaged in the arts in any way, and that the more sexual partners these artists had, the more creative they became. What made that creativity peak even more was when sex was combined with love. This made me feel better, because my research went on to find this statement[75]:

> *The more creative you are, the more sexual partners you should have.*
> *Now I understand why so many people want to be a creative director!*

LOL. Like, LOLOLOLOLOLOLOLOL!!!!! LMFAO. Boy, does this sound like a statement by someone who was fired from an advertising job. Don't worry BK, I am not taking this as gospel. And being a Creative Director is not all unicorns and rainbows. This statement is, however, direct proof that the creative agency business has far too many horny 20-something guys queuing up around the block to work on the next misogynistic Superbowl fart joke commercial. #makeitstop

74 http://news.nationalgeographic.com/news/2005/12/1215_051215_creative_sex.html
75 http://idr.is/sex-and-creativity-do-you-know-their-connections-study-shows-number-of-sexual-partners-correspond-to/

IT CAME. NOW WHAT?

Dealing with the aftermath of an idea

We've learned that creativity and the ideation process is really just manifesting something out of nothing – but what happens after this "something" comes to life?

You would think the "elation of creation" would be at its peak. But for many people, manifesting an idea and releasing it into the wild for all to see can have a much less than satisfying effect.

Full frontal exposure

We've all heard the term "tortured soul" when it comes to describing the manic behavior of some artists. Sylvia Plath committed suicide. Ernest Hemingway was a known raging alcoholic, as was Ludwig Von Beethoven, who was also rumored to suffer from bipolar disorder. Since "mad genius" has been talked about in history – at least when it comes to the creative arts – the notion of being on the side of crazy and savant go hand and hand.

According to Adrienne Sussman, in her Stanford Journal of Neuroscience paper, the traits of creativity are descriptively similar to some of the side effects of mental illness – in fact, the neurological brain states are actually the same.

"Creative thinking, like manic depression and schizophrenia, also involves unusual frontal lobe activity. Frontal lobe deficits may decrease idea generation, in part because of rigid judgments about an idea's worth."

She continues, saying "More than the same brain region, the same neurotransmitters in that region seem to be responsible in both mental illness and creativity. Atypical dopamine levels can not only cause schizophrenic symptoms, but also influence novelty seeking and creative drive. In this way, both the physical and chemical evidence suggest that mental illness and creativity are extremely similar states of mind, if not identical."

This. Is CRAZY. Or should I say, This. Is CREATIVITY.

Does this mean these terms should be interchangeable? Try it at work sometime. Say you think one of your co-workers is completely off their rocker, and in your next meeting they suggest an idea that is out of left field and makes no sense. What if, instead of thinking "Oh my God, this person is a lunatic. They are crazy!" you thought, "Oh my God, this person is a genius. They are so creative!" Who knows what could happen? What if that person's idea was manifested, and something unexpectedly awesome came of it? How many missed opportunities have passed us by because there's such a fine line between brilliance and crazy? Mmmmm. Probably not.

As I believe everyone is creative in their own way, I certainly don't believe that everyone is also mentally ill. OK, like 90%. But there is a nice chunk of people who have pretty creative ideas that get produced, made or published, and they still feel a sense of letdown after the process is finished. What explains that? "When you finish a project at work you're kind of like, 'That was great, but now what?' Your purpose is kind of zapped," says Caroline Beaton. Our familiar culprit frontal lobe is once again to blame. F. Diane Barth, L.C.S.W. and author of Daydreaming: Unlock the Creative Power of Your Mind explains that idealization and disillusionment in life is completely normal.[77] "A sense of everything being special is how we get ourselves into new situations," Barth explains. "It's also a reaction to the flow of natural chemicals, like endorphins, through our bodies that occurs when we get excited about something. The 'high' feeling colors our view of what we see, makes things look maybe better than they would look otherwise, and by doing so, gets us to take those early steps towards development. And then reality steps in. Eventually, the high wears off, the endorphins and other 'feel good' chemicals stop surging through our bodies, and we start to look at things more realistically. As the good feelings dissipate, we start to feel a physical letdown as well as a psychological one. 'Meh' replaces 'Wow!'"

AFTER ANY EXCITING MOMENT, THERE HAS TO BE A LET DOWN. ~F. DIANE BARTH

Ups and downs. Peaks and valleys. Highs and lows. As Barth says, "After any exciting moment, there has to be a let down." <- Literally #TWSS.

Are you seeing a pattern here? This is life, in a nutshell, and our brains are hardwired with chemicals to help us navigate these situations we really like and want to chase, versus those that make us feel terrible about ourselves. How amazing is it that our brains create emotions triggered by situations that provide context to our own continued development of identity and sense of self? To me, this is absolute proof that when you're doing things you love and enjoy, you feel happier, others feel it too, and this energy and excitement is contagious.

Try not to let these post-creative let downs make you think that you've failed, or that you're weird. You can't help it; it's the cocktail shaker in the front of your brain just telling you to go find another party, because it's called happy hour for a reason!

Double D's in the Shower

Good news for creativity and sex lovers alike! The shower seems to be a pretty popular place to do both. I've talked a bit about why ideas seem to naturally surface more in the shower than anywhere else. There's a chemical and environmental reason as to why humans do their best work wet and naked: The "Double D's" themselves, Dopamine and Disengagement.

According to biochemistry, Dopamine is "a compound present in the body as a neurotransmitter and a precursor of other substances including epinephrine." But if you hear others describe it, it's much more omnipresent and desired in our brains than science can communicate. Bethany Brookshire, a post-doctoral student at University of Pennsylvania says that Dopamine is the molecule behind all our most sinful behaviors and secret cravings. "Dopamine is love. Dopamine is lust. Dopamine is adultery. Dopamine is motivation. Dopamine is attention. Dopamine is feminism. Dopamine is addiction,"[78] she says. This particular neurotransmitter in our human brains is, in a way, the "Pavlovian reward system" to things that make us feel pleasure. Or at least that make us feel something. The more we're stimulated, the more Dopamine is released, rewarding us for stimulating the part of our brain where it's released. And, interestingly, this is just one of five receptors contained within this complex neurotransmitter, the others ranging from nausea to kidney function to psychosis to ceasing the production of breast milk (or if you want an easy way to remember it, Dopamine = YES + I'm gonna hurl + I have to pee + All kinds of crazy + boobies).

The second half to this dynamic duo is disengagement, or distraction. This means any environment where your brain isn't required to focus or fixate on any one input, but

78 http://www.slate.com/articles/health_and_science/science/2013/07/what_is_dopamine_love_lust_sex_addiction_gambling_motivation_reward.html

instead is able to relinquish its functionality to a more passive state. The shower is one of those places, producing both a warm, comfortable environment as well as white noise, which helps our minds disengage. "Typical triggers for events, that make us feel great and relaxed and therefore give us an increased dopamine flow are taking a warm shower, exercising, driving home, etc. The chances of having great ideas then are a lot higher," says Leo Widrich, Founder and COO at social sharing app Buffer. "So this seems to be the magic combination: If you are in a relaxed state of mind, easy to distract and full of dopamine, your brain is most likely to give you your best, most creative ideas."[79]

The aftermath of sex: The spawn

Two pink lines. A fun country song, and also a sight that will send you into either a fit of joyful tears or a full-on panic attack. I myself have two kids; a girl, Emerson, who at the time of this writing is in her freshman year of college, and Henry, in 7th grade. Bryan and I have managed to maintain a business, write books, and travel the world while raising them amidst the chaos of Silicon Valley – with the help of quite a few people. It really does take a village to raise kids these days, and it's not easy at all.

Little could prepare you for the creativity it requires to be a parent. The positive problem solving skills one needs to navigate precarious and unexpected situations is off the charts.

Here are a few examples of situations with our kids that activated the chemistry in our frontal lobes:

[Bryan, when Henry was 6 months old]:

[Bryan]: "Court, what's the best way to get throw-up off of Henry?"

[me]: "Oh no, is he sick?"

[Bryan]: "Nope, I puked on him while changing his diaper."

79 https://blog.bufferapp.com/why-we-have-our-best-ideas-in-the-shower-the-science-of-creativity

U - R SO
WYERD

FRUM HYNRY
2 momY

[Bryan with Emerson, at Toys R Us when she was 3]:

> *[Em]: "Can I get two Barbies?"*
>
> *[Bryan]: "No, just one today."*
>
> *[Em]: (a long pause) "Hey, I was wondering… have YOU ever had a Barbie?"*
>
> *[Bryan]: "No, I can't say that I ever have."*
>
> *[Em]: "Well, then you should get a Barbie, and then our Barbie's could play together. That's a good idea!"*
>
> *[Bryan]: (another long pause) "Um… I can't argue with that logic. I guess I'm getting a Barbie."*
>
> *[Em]: "My Barbie wants this one as a friend. Here, let's go pay."*

#FML. In the very best way.

What happens if it doesn't come?

Nothing can shake a human's confidence like feeling like they're unfuckable. Experiencing a "dry spell", when it comes to sex,can be confusing for single and married people alike. In my personal opinion, it's responsible for at least 50% of the bad moods, jerky behavior and crying fits in the human population.

Aside from feeling like you've regained your virginity, or that you need to vacuum for cobwebs down there, going for long spells of no sex can have real health side effects. We outlined the benefits of having a lot of sex earlier, but not having it can have the completely opposite effect too. A lower immune system, more intense PMS, and, according to website madamenoire.com, "swampy secretions". #ew

It's not all bad news though. At least for women, it's been reported that in times of a sexual drought, we channel our energy into work instead, increasing our productivity[81].

80 http://madamenoire.com/599839/time-knock-dust-off-consequences-going-without-sex-long/5/

❧ THESE GO BOTH WAYS ❧

ANYONE WHO IS A PARENT UNDERSTANDS THAT
THESE PHRASES, SAID MOST LIKELY ON A DAILY BASIS TO
YOUR KIDS, ARE ALL EQUALLY APPLICABLE TO SEX.

- WHY IS THIS STICKY?

- WHERE ARE YOUR PANTS?

- I NEED YOU TO TAKE ONE MORE BITE
WITHOUT GAGGING.

- JUST PUT IT IN YOUR MOUTH.

- WILL YOU TAKE A SHOWER ALREADY?

- STOP THAT BANGING!

- WHEN CAN I PICK YOU UP?

- WHY ARE YOU SQUIRMING?

I guess we know what the procrastinators of the world have been doing!

I'll tell you who doesn't get it: this guy[81]. He asks, "What about when things don't go so well for a while? Say you suffer a couple of rough nights out. Maybe a load of mediocre women didn't want to speak to you or perhaps, your girlfriend dumped you. It's natural for this to affect your confidence, which will in turn impact your overall attractiveness to the opposite sex."

WOW. A "mediocre" woman? The measurement standard here equating a breakup with your girlfriend to that of being rejected by a 5/10. I am sure in his head, we women stand around saying things like "Hey Janet, your hair looks extra shiny tonight, I hope the guys notice it in the dim bar lighting and see you've upped your game from 'mediocre' to 'hot'." #Saidnowomanever

This article reads like a Jack Handy skit from Saturday Night Live. I hope the author has located his confidence, but I think he's looking for it in the wrong place. While he's focused on creating a "reality a hot woman would want to be a part of," he should be consuming massive doses of humility instead.

81 http://elitedaily.com/dating/how-to-get-over-sex-drought/1033841/?utm_source=huffingtonpost&utm_medium=tr&utm_campaign=p10k80

ASK MORE QUESTIONS

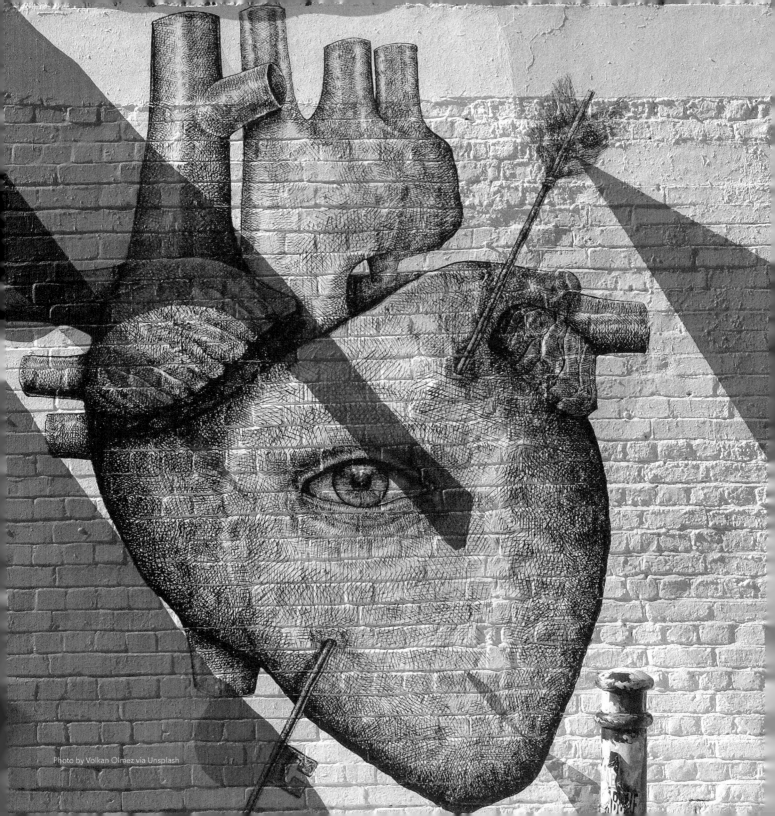

LOVE IN. LOVE OUT.

I can feel it back, because, you know… science

As far back as Plato and Sir Isaac Newton, curious thinkers have been trying to scientifically explain why "like" things are attracted to "like" things.

In modern Quantum Physics, the Law of Attraction states that since we now understand the energetic makeup of humans at a molecular level, that the amount of thought, and what you're thinking about, is what attracts the manifestation of that thought energy in return. John Assaraf, author of bestselling book *Having It All,* describes it this way: "Our thoughts are linked to this [our personal experiences] invisible energy and they determine what the energy forms. Your thoughts literally shift the universe on a particle-by-particle basis to create your physical life.[82]"

So knowing what we know about the Law of Attraction, could the same be true about what we manifest for others?

Whatever you're doing in your life, whether you're a teacher or truck driver or a CEO or anything in this world, people feel the amount of energy and love that you put into whatever you do. They feel it back, and it has a direct effect on how much they engage, share, react, respond, and remember, everything that you're doing. Remember this; If you phone it in, no one's going to answer.

We call this "Love in/Love out", meaning the amount of love (focused, positive, energy) you put into an idea is directly felt back by the receiver when they experience its physical manifestation.

I can't explain how it works, but the Universe is consistent with it. So don't skimp on the energy you put into an idea, because there's no getting around the Universe!

#Ikindafeellikeishouldmakeamoodboardnow

The Math Part

When I was pregnant with my son, I went an entire year without drinking a single drop of booze. Great for the baby – but even better for my brain cells! My thinking went into overdrive, and at the time in 2004, the web was still pretty young. Our clients were relatively inexperienced marketers and small business owners, and I spent quite a bit of my time trying to convince them why they should market instead of what they should be doing for their business. #exhausting Anyway, at the time, I was also judging quite a few creative competitions, the kind where you lend your expertise by assigning a score to a piece of work.

THE MORE ENERGY YOU GIVE AN IDEA, THE MORE PEOPLE FEEL IT BACK.

This got me thinking. What if you could predict the amount of visitor traffic to your website by using a combination of science and spirit? I used a simple ratio:

$$\frac{\text{Current score of site (design, writing, tone, user experience, functionality)}}{\text{Current site traffic}} = \frac{\text{Optimal score of site}}{\text{X (new site traffic)}}$$

For illustrative purposes, let's assume that each criteria holds a value of 10. So, a website that was in dire need of an overhaul would have scores that looked like this:

- Design: 2
- Writing: 3
- Tone: 2
- User Experience: 1
- Site total: 8/40

Pretty dismal, right?

If their current site traffic was, say, 2500 unique visitors/month, the equation would look like this:

$$\frac{8}{2500} = \frac{40}{X}$$

When you cross multiply, you get 8x = 100,000

Divide 100K by 8, and X= 12,500

So, my theory suggests that by creating an optimal experience with this company's website, they would increase their site traffic 5x simply by optimizing to 10 each category in the criteria.

I got to test out this theory on an actual client project – once. And you know what? I'll be damned if their site traffic prediction didn't net out to be within less than 100 site visits in the first month. Genius? Or pure friggin luck?!

I drink now, so we'll never know.

I'm attracted to this

Applying the "Law of Attraction" to human relationships was made popular in 2006 by Esther and Jerry Hicks in their book by the same title, then exploded when Rhonda Byrne's documentary "The Secret", was featured on Oprah. 'The Secret' simply connects the Universal Law of Attraction to our own human thoughts: When your energy, or thoughts, focus on what you want, and your actions align with these thoughts, you raise your vibration to attract "like" things that vibrate at the same energetic frequency.

BE A HUMAN VIBRATOR AND YOU'LL BE MUCH HAPPIER. BUT YOU HAVE TO BE TURNED ON FOR IT TO WORK.

It sounds so simple, right? Like, so simple that it couldn't ever work because it's too simple. BAH! I believe life was created to be simple, we just over complicate everything around it because of our fears, or because we need stuff to do, or because we need to feel needed, or there's nothing on TV.

For most of us, it's too scary to just – let – go.

For me too. But I'm working on it everyday, and you can too.

It stands to reason that if the power of pointed, intentful thinking can return the outcomes we want, why couldn't it work for other things as well?

Look into my eyes

In the 18th century, the practice of studying "Animal Magnetism", or "Mesmerism" (the name given to the practice by the German doctor Franz Mesmer) was a common thing. Dr. Mesmer observed an invisible energy force exerted between animals that produced

83 http://www.joydavidson.com/sex-and-the-secret-how-the-law-of-attraction-can-transform-your-sex-life/

physical properties, including healing. His theory sparked a magnetic healing movement in Vienna and Paris in the late 18th century whose practitioners were called "magnetizers", feeding their subjects large does of iron and then running their hands over their bodies while holding magnets. Sometimes they would massage the affected areas as well.

Hmmmmm. :/

Today, magnetism is not recognized as part of medical science. But although it was denounced as more of the power of suggestion rather than real science, it is recognized as laying the groundwork in the United States for modern-day hypnosis and psychotherapy. Given its roots in improving dispositions and self-confidence, it served as the first secular form of treatment that combined spirit with well-being. According to Psychologist Philip Cushman, "It was an ambitious attempt to combine religion with psychotherapy, and it spawned ideologies such as mind cure philosophy, the New Thought movement, Christian Science and American spiritualism."

In other words, they did it missionary style.

Speaking of missionary style...

Dr. Joy Davidson, a few years ago, developed seven ways the Law of Attraction could be used to improve your sex life[83]. She also believes in the Secret, so the Universe is on her side, which makes me sure these will work.

Here is a short version of her list:

Mind Magic: How to Use the Law Of Attraction to Make Sex Sizzle

Think about your desired sex life in strictly positive terms. Say, "I want an orgasm every day "- not, I want my partner to stop being so selfish in bed.

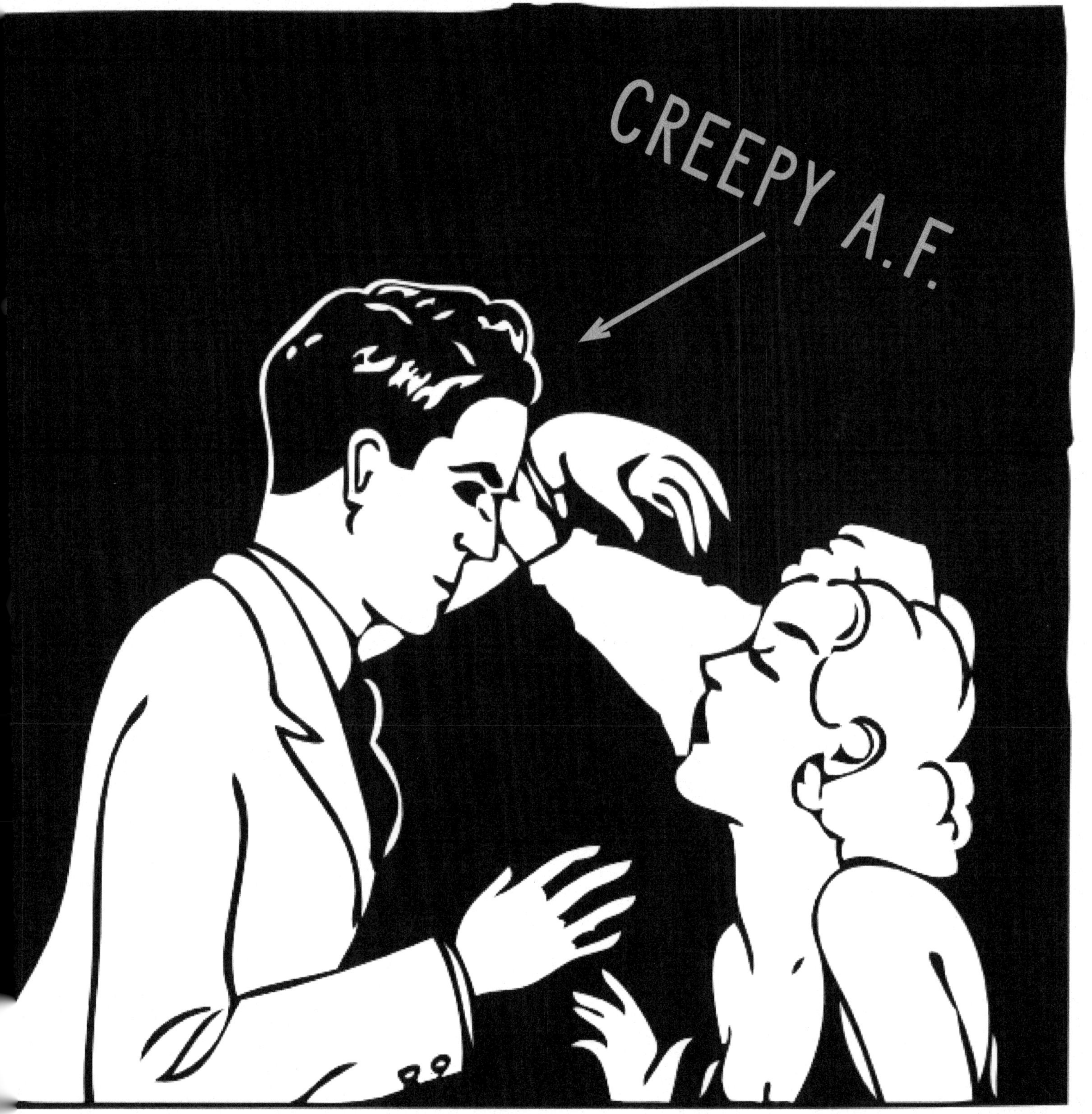
CREEPY A.F.

See yourself as already having the things you want (a million dollar toy chest?) and being sexual in the ways you want to be: fearlessly, adventurously, or spiritually.

You are already who you want to be. Focus there and the extraneous will peel away, freeing you.

Pay attention to your thoughts before falling asleep. Focus on what you want to manifest in your life.

Visualize, using color and motion. See yourself jumping up and down and exclaiming joyously over the thrilling sexual experiences you're having.

Focus on the emotion of being excited and aroused.

Actively change the aspects of your life that contradict your desired goals. If you want to be seen as a siren, but you always wear mommy underwear, you're telling the universe that you appreciate being seen as mommy, not as a sex symbol. Trash the cotton briefs and buy fresh lingerie that speaks to the part of you that has been hiding. Treat yourself like a siren and the rest of the world will follow.

Note to self: Buy new underwear, stat! And this doesn't just apply to women, here is some lingerie for men[84]. #Strangelyhot

84 http://www.huffingtonpost.com/entry/mens-lingerie_us_56a92080e4b0f7179928d6e3?te=R29

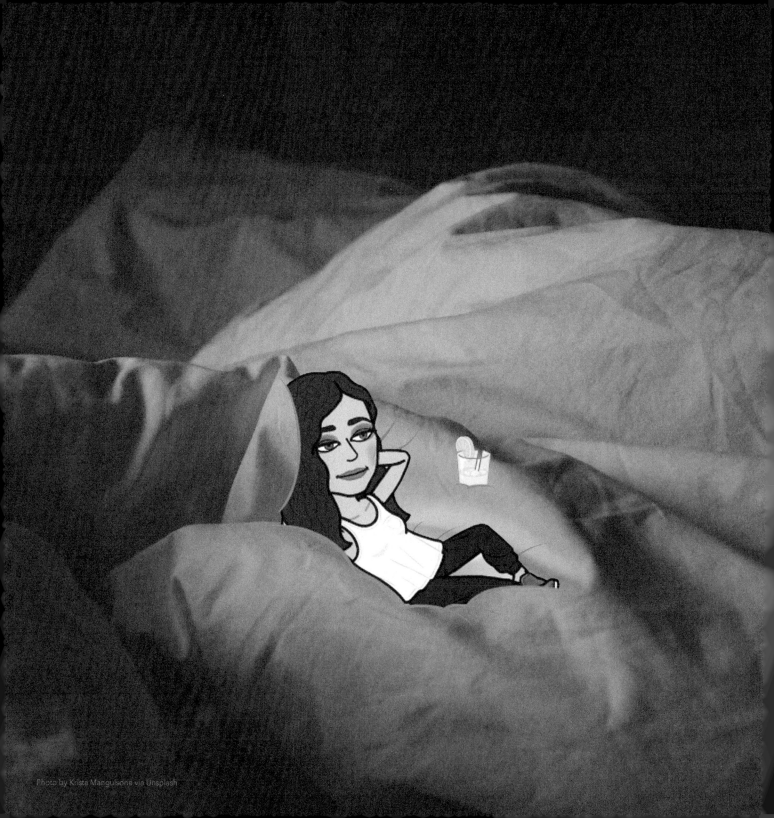

OH YES, DON'T STOP

This ending may need massaging

Many of you have heard the term "Happy Ending", referring to being on the receiving end of a handy by a masseuse after a massage. It is legal in some Asian countries, and although illegal in the United States, the lines are blurring as more inexpensive "pop-up" (LOL, see what I did there) massage spas appear on the scene. If you're a massage therapist, it seems like it would be a lot of work to do, and awkward afterwards, especially if you're a guy since there's only one big sheet and no towel #ew #whyisthatsticky

The real Happy Ending

After all of my research, talking to people with diverse careers, approaches, philosophies, and backgrounds, I found that a common theme emerged about creativity. In as much as I set out to write this book to show that just like sex, every single human is creative in their own way, I was more reminded that creativity is our most unique human way of connecting with each other. How we do that – through artistry, or solution finding, or storytelling, or, or or – is up to us. The vehicles we choose to connect with other humans – writing, music, film, science, math, fashion, programming… hell, even restocking shelves – are as varied as snowflakes.

So, if all you did was pick up this book and flip to the last page to see if you actually wanted to read it, here's all you need to know:

- At the end of the day, it's about love and connection with others.

- Enjoy the moment and the power of the space you create.

- Laugh, and work at making others laugh.

- Kick your own Monsieur Non in the crotch daily. (OK, you *will* have to read the book to get this.)

- We're only here for an eyelash's amount of time in the spectrum of life, so why the hell waste it on boring meaningless stuff?!

- Commit to a lifetime of creativity, and a lifetime of great sex.

- If you're reading this, you can do it, and yes, never, ever stop.

All of these feel really fucking good… so massage your creativity, always. That's a happy ending I'm willing to get behind, for sure. #TWSS

THE BEGINNING

DESIGN

HERE'S MY HASHTAG: #CREATIVITYISLIKESEX

CONNECT WITH ME:

TWITTER + SNAPCHAT @CSHASARRIVED

INSTAGRAM @CSMITHPM

FACEBOOK /COURTNEYSMITHKRAMER

COURTNEY SMITH KRAMER

An accomplished creative strategist, storyteller, writer and designer, Courtney has a knack for simplifying the complex and has been told she has a wicked sense of humor. She began her career as an art director in East Lansing, MI in 1991, and then subsequently ran a successful design firm, which she owned and operated for three years. In 2002, Courtney relocated to San Jose, California and co-founded PureMatter with her husband, Bryan Kramer, where she currently serves as creative and strategic lead for its Fortune 500 clients.

Courtney has collectively earned hundreds of creative awards and her work has appeared in the PRINT International Design Annual, Logo Lounge Master Library Series and Graphic Design Monthly. She is an accomplished national creative juror for the AIVA (Academy of Interactive and Visual Arts), and has juried the Creativity International Competition, the W3 Awards sponsored by Adweek, and numerous American Advertising Federation (AAF) ADDY Awards and National Student Advertising Competitions (NSAC) across the country. Courtney is a former Governor of the AAF District 14 and currently sits as an Advisory Board member for the World Brand Congress.

Author's note: It's weird to talk about yourself in the third person. I like to laugh and drink wine, that's pretty much all you need to know.

I AM HUMAN.
I HAVE AN IMAGINATION,
AND THAT ALLOWS ME TO
BE UNIQUELY CREATIVE
AT ANYTHING I CARE
ABOUT.

LOVE, YOU.

CPSIA information can be obtained
at www.ICGtesting.com
Printed in the USA
FSOW04n2328051017
39306FS